HIGH-POWERED
Plyometrics

JAMES C. RADCLIFFE, MS
ROBERT C. FARENTINOS, PhD

Human Kinetics

Library of Congress Cataloging–in–Publication Data

Radcliffe, James C. (James Christopher), 1958–
    High-powered plyometrics / James C. Radcliffe, Bob C. Farentinos.
      p.   cm.
    Includes bibliographical references (p.) and index.
    ISBN 0-88011-784-2
    1. Plyometrics.   I. Farentinos, Robert C., 1941–   . II. Title.
  GV711.5.R326   1999
  613.7'1—dc21   98–52761
                                                  CIP

ISBN 0-88011-784-2

Acquisitions Editor: Martin Barnard
Developmental Editor: Anne Heiles
Assistant Editor: John Wentworth
Copyeditor: Denelle Eknes
Proofreader: Sue Fetters
Graphic Designers: George Amaya and Brian McElwain
Graphic Artist: Brian McElwain
Cover Designer: Jack Davis
Cover photographer: Oscar Palmquist
Interior photographer: Oscar Palmquist
Illustrators: Kim Maxey and Sharon Smith
Printer: United Graphics

Printed in the United States of America   10 9 8 7 6 5 4 3 2 1

Web site: http://www.humankinetics.com/

United States: Human Kinetics
P.O. Box 5076
Champaign, IL 61825-5076
1-800-747-4457
e-mail: humank@hkusa.com

Canada: Human Kinetics
475 Devonshire Road Unit 100
Windsor, ON N8Y 2L5
1-800-465-7301 (in Canada only)
e-mail: humank@hkcanada.com

Europe: Human Kinetics, P.O. Box IW14
Leeds LS16 6TR, United Kingdom
(44) 1132 781708
e-mail: humank@hkeurope.com

Australia: Human Kinetics
57A Price Avenue
Lower Mitcham, South Australia 5062
(088) 277 1555
e-mail: humank@hkaustralia.com

New Zealand: Human Kinetics
P.O. Box 105-231, Auckland 1
(09) 523 3462
e-mail: humank@hknewz.com

Contents

Foreword

Perhaps one of the most exciting training innovations of the past 25 years has been plyometric training. Coaches and athletes were quick to realize its potential for improving athletic performance. What was missing was a systematic approach to its application. Where did it fit into the whole program? How much was enough? What was the proper intensity and volume? What exercises were most effective? What about periodization—where did it fit best into the training year? Was it appropriate for use with the younger athlete? Was it as effective with the female athlete? What was the scientific basis of the training method? These were all legitimate questions that needed to be answered to make the method viable for training.

As with any training innovation there was much mystique and some confusion surrounding the method. Much of this occurred because plyometrics was first portrayed as a secret Russian training method. In reality, plyometric training was not a particularly new training method, nor was it the exclusive domain of the Russian sport machine. What was new was the term "plyometrics," which first appeared in coaching literature in the late 1960s. Before that it was called "jump training." It was used for years throughout the world without notable results, due to the lack of a systematic approach. Then in the 1960s the success of the Russian high jumpers and triple jumpers created an interest in the systematic approach to the application of the method.

Also lacking had been a good foundation in sport science research. Beginning in the late 1950s and continuing on today, the landmark research into the scientific foundations of the method has been done in the former Soviet Union (Verkhoshansky), Finland (Komi), Germany (Schmidtbleicher), Italy (Margaria and Bosco), and lately Australia (Wilson and Newton). The work of these researchers has given us a fundamental understanding of the elastic properties of muscle and its trainability, which has enabled the practitioner to systematically apply plyometrics for the improvement of explosive power.

Despite the research foundations, plyometrics has been trivialized and become a buzzword because of poor methodology and training design. Plyometric training is specific work for the enhancement of explosive power. It is not a general fitness activity. It is highly specialized. It is a training method to be used in conjunction with other power-development methods in a complete training program to improve the relationship between maximum strength and explosive power. It is not a stand-alone training method. For maximum effectiveness it must be trained in conjunction with other power-development methods. Correct basic technique in execution of the exercises, proper progression, and periodization must be emphasized for maximum effectiveness. Otherwise there is a higher risk of injury and minimal training return.

I was honored when Jim Radcliffe asked me to write the foreword to his new book. His first plyometrics book was a landmark because it was the first written in any language that addressed the concept of plyometric training in a systematic manner and its specific application to sports performance. Subsequent editions of the book further defined the method and its application. Now this book begins where all other books on the subject have left off. There is a significant amount of new information that reflects current research and the accumulation of practical field experience in day-to-day work with athletes in a cross-section of sports. It addresses a serious need for precise terminology to facilitate communication and eliminate confusion. This is coupled with a sound methodological approach emphasizing precise technical execution of the exercises as well as a specific order and progression to the drills to minimize risk of injury and maximize the training benefit. The title tells it all—it is about explosive power training that is optimized through a planned performance program design approach. *High-Powered Plyometrics* underscores the potential that plyometric training has as an integral training component for all sports that require explosive power.

—Vern Gambetta

Preface: Finding What You Want in This Book

Our objective in presenting *High-Powered Plyometrics* is not modest—we aim to provide the most systematic, comprehensive, and practical treatment of plyometrics available. This book is the most complete work on this style of training, providing concepts, practical information, training, and performance evaluation.

During the last 15 years we have conducted an extensive program of plyometric training for fitness enthusiasts and high school and college athletes. Intercollegiate and professional football and basketball players, world-class cross-country skiers, weightlifters, cyclists, track athletes, marathon and mountain runners, young athletes, and older fitness buffs have trained in plyometrics, among them several participants in the Olympic games and World Championships throughout the 1980s and 1990s. *High-Powered Plyometrics* is the result of research and coaching, and especially of Jim's original and practical work during the past two decades.

We wrote this book for coaches, athletes, sports medicine clinicians, and all who wish to know more about plyometrics and how to apply this dynamic training method to specific sports. We have expanded the original version to include comprehensively defined training concepts, thorough teaching and training methodologies, and the latest research and practical considerations. A 50-minute videotape complements this book.

We are deeply committed to plyometric training: we use it in our own workouts and in directing the training of others. We have extensively reviewed the professional literature in this area of training and present these findings along with our experiences. Many other books give good definitions of plyometric training and descriptions of how to set up the training and perform certain exercises. *High-Powered Plyometrics*, however, is the first and most complete work on the principles of establishing training regimes and optimally progressing throughout specific exercise sequences for enhanced training and performance.

The term *plyometrics* has been derived from the Greek word *pleythyein*, meaning "to augment" or "to increase," and the shorter Greek words *plio* "more" and *plyo* "to move." Metrics means "to measure" or "length." The spelling pliometric is also accepted in referring to eccentric contraction or muscle lengthening. The word *plyometrics* originally appeared in Russian sports literature in 1966 in work completed by V.M. Zaciorskij (Zanon 1989). An American track and field coach named Fred Wilt offered explanation of the term in 1975, and many have followed. A few other terms have been associated with plyometrics as well, including shock training, speed strength, bounce training, and elastic reactivity.

Although we know some basic neuromuscular processes underlying plyometrics, we must learn a great deal more before we fully understand how it works. Fortunately, that continuing research is underway, conducted by such sport scientists as Yuri Verkhoshansky, Carmelo Bosco, Paavo Komi, Gregory Wilson, Mel Siff, Maarten Bobbert, Warren Young, Vern Gambetta, James Hay, and others (see References and Suggested Readings). From a practical viewpoint, experience supports the significant value of plyometrics, even if, from a physiological perspective, you find perplexing the explanations for why the training and performance of plyometrics work.

The constant struggle to be practical yet scientifically accurate is a commonplace experience in physical training. Every day we coaches and athletes try to do the things that will give us the best results. We want to be efficient, and we would like the results to be reliable. This book will facilitate the clinical understanding of why you can expect certain results from explosive training, yet not have to be in the lab to do so.

To understand what is happening when you perform these training methods, turn to chapter 1, which will give you the background for what is happening inside and why. This chapter defines plyometrics, presents concepts, and describes the principles of how and why plyometrics works.

If you want to find out if you or your participants are ready to use the training methods, or how to get ready, turn to chapter 2. The best training and results will come from those methods you use properly, not just explosively, but overall. In this chapter we describe the elements involved with preparing for training and performance: equipment and basic types of exercises.

Chapter 3 gives the guidelines for training safely and successfully. This chapter contains information on necessary training elements and safety precautions you need to perform skillfully in sports as well as the principles for executing plyometric exercises.

Chapters 4, 5, and 6 are the handbook of training exercises. A field guide of training drills and demonstrations, chapters 4 and 5 describe basic plyometrics movements related to various areas of the body: legs, trunk, and arms. In chapter 6 we get more specific, showing you how to apply drill sequences to athletic activities in particular sports. This chapter gives specific workout cards to use on the field, court, or track.

You can learn about seeking advancement, planning for elite performances, and peaking at the right time and place by referring to chapter 7. This chapter is a new section, giving more technical discussion on evaluations, periodization, and long-term planning.

Finally, we give you a plan to continue with plyometric training at the most advanced levels. We also tell you how to use *progression,* an aspect of plyometrics necessary at every workout level and in every athletic situation. In addition to chapters devoted to this aspect, we describe each drill in the proper progressive manner. Over 200 sequential photographs enhance the concepts, descriptions, and explanations.

Acknowledgments

We are grateful to several people who have helped us with this book: Farentinos Gym members and coaches, especially Mike Lopez, who helped Jim Radcliffe with his initial endeavors in the plyometric area. We received valuable assistance from Greg Bezer, Harvey Newton, Ed Burke, Don Nielsen, Audun Endestad, Pat Ahern, Dave Felkley, Dan Allen, Steve Ilg, John Tansley, I.J. Gorman, Steven and Chris Farentinos, Vern Gambetta, Robb Rogers, Carmelo Bosco, Mark Stream, Lou Osternig, Janice Lettunich Radcliffe, Pat Lombardi, Geoff Ginther, Dave Ziemba, Oscar Palmquist, Aisha Wallace, Sue Morris, and the many athletes and coaches from the University of Oregon in Eugene.

We have enjoyed the personal and professional associations with all concerned and truly hope we have returned the favor in some way.

Chapter 1

The Science in Plyometrics

Plyometrics is a method of developing explosive power. It is also an important component of most athletic performances. As coaches and athletes have recognized the potential improvements plyometrics can bring to performance, they have integrated it into the overall training program in many sports and made it a significant factor in planning the scope of athletic development.

Power

Although the exact reasons that plyometrics works may still hold some mystery, it is a fact that the training brings results. Yuri Verkhoshansky had stated in the late 1960s that individuals could significantly improve jumping and sprinting ability by progressive jumping exercises. The suggested training and performances of athletes such as Olympic sprint champion Valeri Borzov helped to substantiate those statements. In the early 1980s, researchers Russ Polhemus, Ed Burkhardt, and others offered substantial evidence that combining plyometric training with a weight-training program enhanced physical development far beyond that of weight-training programs alone. You can enhance strength and speed, and avoid injury with good combined programming.

People have probably always valued physical power, and, at least since the times of the ancient Greeks, athletes have sought methods for improving their speed and strength. Power, after all, is the combination of strength and speed, force times velocity. Power is the application of force through a range of motion within a unit of time.

Power is essential in performing most sport skills, whether a tennis serve or a clean and jerk. Not surprisingly, then, specific exercises have long been designed to enhance quick, explosive movements. Yet it is only in the last few decades that several programs have been developed to systematically emphasize explosive-reactive power. It is still more recent that training to develop explosive power has been refined.

Progress in this area of knowledge now hinges on two complications. First, several methods exist to develop explosive or reactive power (or both). Some are general, others more specific, and each has distinct characteristics. The second complication is that these methods have been researched, developed, practiced, and interpreted in several different countries, languages, and structures of society. In this chapter we will give a broad view of the interpretations to help you understand the system of training. Rather than go into depth here about the scientific area, we will discuss the most important principles and refer you to scientific research available elsewhere (see References and Suggested Readings).

At the foundation of the comprehensive training you will find in this book are a few principles whose effectiveness is clear from experience. One is using to full advantage the power from eccentric contractions. A second is the advantage you gain from exploiting the stretch-shortening cycle (SSC) and the explosive power available from the elastic components of muscle. A third is to adapt to plyometrics programs the underlying soundness of the training principles of progressive overload and specificity.

Muscle Contractions

The human body is continually subject to external forces and impacts, against which muscles contract. Their contractions (or *actions,* a term preferred by some physiologists) are both negative (*eccentric*) and positive (*concentric*). In eccentric contractions, the muscles undergo tension and lengthen or stretch (called *negative work*); in concentric contractions they undergo tension and shorten (called *positive work*). Any external force a muscle experiences that is greater than its internal tension force allows it to lengthen in an eccentric contraction. This type of contraction enables the muscle to brake skeletal movements, in other words, to decelerate. An *eccentric contraction* allows a muscle to sustain greater tension than it can develop in an isometric position. Because the load applied to the muscle causes it to work by lengthening, it is called negative work (in contrast to the positive work done in *concentric contraction* to overcome resistance). That is, when muscles contract eccentrically, they lengthen as they simultaneously produce force. The external load is greater than the internal muscular force it can apply. Basically, every movement in the direction of gravity is under the control of an eccentric contraction.

What is significant here is that the energy cost of the negative work is less than that of positive work. The body requires less motor-unit activation and consumes less oxygen in eccentric contractions and exercise compared with concentric contractions. Thus, there is a different relationship between input and output of energy—a higher mechanical efficiency in eccentric than in concentric exercise.

In eccentric actions performed at moderate to high speeds, the muscles call on fast-twitch motor units to work; these fast-twitch muscle-fiber units are thus preferentially recruited. They have higher firing frequencies and are larger fibers, producing more force per motor unit than other muscle-fiber types. Force production during eccentric contraction is greater than concentric contractions because the body generates a higher tension at the point of the muscle's insertion. The tendon at insertion receives larger loads during eccentric than during concentric exercise.

In summary, because of chemical, mechanical, and neurological factors that influence the force and stiffness of the contracting muscle (see Komi 1973), eccentric lengthening (before rapid concentric shortening) produces the greatest force and power capabilities in skeletal muscle. It is therefore the central type of contraction to plyometrics.

Loading and the Stretch Response

A muscle's initial length when it is stimulated influences the magnitude of its contractile responses to a stimulus. Applying force against a muscle, or *loading*, causes a reaction to the stress. When you apply this load, the amount of deformation (called *strain)* is the change that occurs in dimension. An internal liquid within the muscle resists these deformations during stretching and shortening, and this resistance to flow is known as *viscosity*. It is because of the viscosity that muscles must move in the direction opposite the desired force application (this is called *prestretch*). The property of muscle tissue that enables greater muscular tension is known as the *stretch response*. Not to be confused with stretch reflex (a basic neural mechanism to maintain active muscle tonus using impulses discharged from muscle spindles), the stretch response involves parallel muscle fibers exerting maximal tension at stretch lengths slightly greater than resting length.

Elasticity

Muscle strength is the maximum force or tension that a muscle can generate. This is the force or tension a muscle group can exert against a resistance in one maximal effort. An important component accompanying strength is the muscle's *elasticity*, its ability to lengthen and increase in tension, which resides in the contractile elements of skeletal muscle. Naturally, there are limits to these abilities.

The range of elasticity, or strain, is directly proportionate to the ability of the tissue to resist forces and return to its original shape upon releasing a load. It is this elastic property that plyometric training plays on.

Elasticity lends the ability to *use* the strain or tension to return to or react in the original direction with greater force, more efficiency, or both. It is the basis for resilience, or the ability to absorb energy within the elastic range the muscle works. When a load is removed and the tissue returns to its original shape, resilience causes the release of energy.

Studying elasticity has led to the concept of *stored elastic energy,* which is the recoverable energy the viscoelastic tissue deformation generates in the eccentric phase of the movement. This energy is available for reuse in the following concentric phase of muscle activity. Elastic energy has also been explained as mechanical energy that the muscle does not dissipate as heat, but rather absorbs and stores for reuse during its subsequent, active, shortening cycle.

Exploiting the Stretch-Shortening Cycle

Eccentric and concentric muscle actions usually occur simultaneously in combinations of muscle function otherwise known as the *stretch-shortening cycle* (SSC). The eccentric contraction stretches a muscle's length, and the concentric contraction shortens it. Most movements result from concentric actions preceded by an eccentric countermovement. Defining the principles of the stretch-shortening cycle will help us understand not only what is occurring within training and performing but also how to apply these principles. This understanding is useful in planning plyometric training.

In analyzing and applying training that uses the stretch-shortening cycle model, remain aware that performance of human athletic skills is never merely the sum of such factors as strength, velocity, loading, and stretch. Performance of any movement pattern, plyometric or otherwise, is holistic in nature. It is an integration of all such factors. In developing human power, many mechanisms drive and coordinate the skeletal musculature. Enhancing muscular control and reactive power associated with the stretch-shortening cycle exercise relates to changes in complex neuromuscular structure and sensory-motor pathways.

Perhaps the most accurate term to describe the time from the eccentric or stretch portion of the cycle through switching to the concentric or shortened portion is *elastic-reactive,* a concept that Vern Gambetta described in 1986. What is important in elastic reactivity is the impulse, or the force that starts a body into motion, and the motion this force produces. Greater impulse relates to better efficiency. When greater stretches precede positive work, they produce increased mechanical efficiency. Called *potentiation* (see Komi 1986), the mechanics explain synergistically augmented energy levels and heightened effectiveness.

The basis of both the voluntary and involuntary motor processes involved in the stretch-shortening cycle is the so-called stretch reflex, which is also called the *muscle spindle reflex* or *myotatic reflex.* This spindle apparatus and the stretch reflex are vital components of the nervous system's overall control of body movement. In executing most movement skills, the muscles receive some type of load. The rapid stretching (loading) of these muscles activates the muscle spindle reflex, which sends a strong stimulus through the spinal cord to the muscles. This stimulus causes them to contract powerfully.

Let's now look briefly at how the stretch-shortening cycle works. Various terms have been suggested to describe phases of the stretch-shortening cycle, which includes the stretch or eccentric phase, the brief period between, and the stretch or concentric phase. Basically, the cycle combines an eccentric contraction, in which the involved muscles undergo tension through lengthening or stretching (negative work), and a concentric contraction, in which the muscles shorten (positive work). Figure 1.1 shows the cycle in its clinical form of muscle function and as it appears in its natural form.

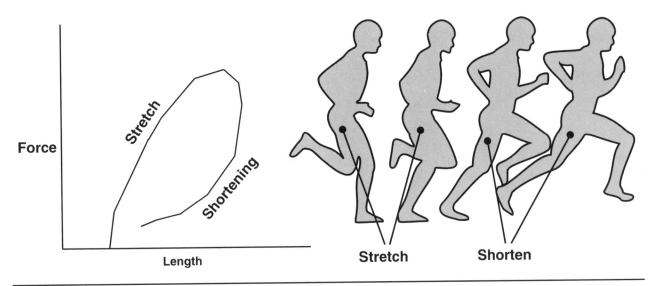

Figure 1.1   The stretch-shortening cycle.

Amortization Phase

As a general term, *amortization* is the gradual extinction, extinguishing, or deadening of something; in the stretch-shortening cycle it refers to the time that elapses from the beginning of the eccentric contraction phase to the beginning of the concentric contraction phase (see figure 1.2).

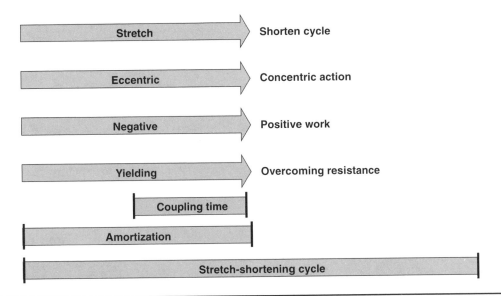

Figure 1.2   Terminology involved with amortization.

Myotatic (Stretch) Reflex

Muscle spindles and other musculoskeletal sensory organs detect muscle stretch, sending impulses to the spinal cord and back for more dynamic contractions.

> ***Concept:*** Place designated muscles under prestretch by working from eccentric to concentric in order to incorporate reflexive responses.

Elastic and Contractile Components

Springlike elements located in series (series elastic component or SEC) or parallel (parallel elastic component or PEC) to the myofilament of skeletal muscle are tension activated (Hill 1950). Muscles store elastic energy during eccentric work and recover it in concentric work. If amortization is slow, muscles dissipate elastic energy, usually as heat (Cavagna 1977). Elasticity is enhanced if the prestretch and exchange duration is minimal (Komi 1973). Researchers believe the rate of stretch to be more important than its length or magnitude. We desire quick prestretch movements over longer, slower ones (Cavagna 1977; Bosco and Komi 1979).

Proprioception and Potentiation

Perceptions of motion are transmitted from muscle to spinal cord, brain, and back to muscle, regulating body movement via musculoskeletal sensory organs, interpretation by the central nervous system, motor unit recruitment, and muscle stiffness.

> ***Concept:*** Training with a prestretch and activating neuromuscular components improves the efficiency of neural actions and muscular performance (Schmidtbleicher 1992).

Exercises that use the stretch-shortening cycle, or plyometrics, stimulate changes in the neuromuscular system, enhancing the ability of the muscle groups to respond more quickly and powerfully to slight and rapid changes in muscle length. An important feature is that the exercises condition the neuromuscular system to allow faster and more powerful changes of direction.

In terms of plyometrics, you can formulate exercises that isolate various sections of the body for training. The exercises involve an array of jumps, bounds, hops; flexions, extensions, trunk rotations; and tossing, throwing, or passing. You'll find descriptions and definitions of these moves later, especially in chapters 4 through 6, and these are merely a beginning to the movements you can devise to exploit the stretch-shortening cycle.

Core of Plyometrics Planning

Certain principles of athletic training apply especially to the stretch-shortening cycle and plyometrics. The first is a basic and widely accepted training principle: progressive overload.

Progressive Overload

Using the principle of progressive overload successfully develops strength, power, and endurance. The relationship between increasing muscular strength and resistive overload using weights is well known. Repetitions of work at less than an overload emphasize endurance of the muscle—not strength.

Because we are emphasizing power development, and because power is the function of force times distance over time, you can use several overload methods. However, rather than the traditional definition of power, strength times speed, the principle of overload exploits the true formula of power in planning your training sessions.

A term often used instead of power training is speed-strength. It indicates the ability to reach the maximum of strength during the movement in a brief time—a ratio of maximum strength in a movement and the time to reach it (Matveyev 1977). Many sport scientists use the term to describe several correlating components of strength: primarily, these are absolute, explosive, starting, and reactive. Perhaps a breakdown in a more definitive formula is appropriate, so let us take another view of power. A basic physics lecture for power always gives the following formula, with these applications:

F = application of force
d = application through the greatest distance
t = application in the least amount of time

$$P = \frac{F \times d}{t}$$

Let's put into words what we are really after:

F = force application (this is strength and impulse)
d = distance transition (this is agility and coordination)
t = time reduction (this is speed and acceleration)

Few coaches would disagree that to apply more force (F) you must have improved strength. Also, few would ignore that reducing the time (t) factor takes accelerated movements. However, surprisingly many coaches neglect to incorporate the formula's other equation—the agility and coordination you need to make appropriate distance transitions (d). The body's characteristics (its size and shape, for example) always set certain limitations, of course. Because you need all three components (each is an important piece) to make up the pie, in plyometric training you must plan to involve overloads that can accomplish what you want in all these areas.

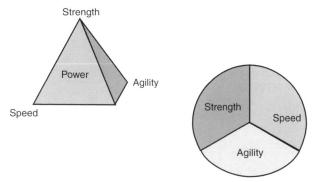

The types of overloads available to plyometric training are shown in the box below.

Plyometric Overloading

Resistive Overload	Spatial Overload	Temporal Overload
• Gravitational	• Range	• Operating rate
• Inclination	• Saggital, tranverse, frontal	• Impulse
• External		

In training the stretch-shortening cycle, resistive overloads usually take the form of rapidly stretching a limb or the entire body in an eccentric contraction, such as overcoming the increased g-forces as the result of falling from a height. You can place a spatial overload on the stretch-shortening cycle by increasing the range, within a desired plane of movement, that the athlete must perform the application of forces. Movement can also have the effects of overload through range of motion. The concept is to emp oy6áhe stretch reflex within a specific range of motion. An example here is of an athlete performing a vertical jump from both feet without any approach. The application of force is upward, with all parts of the body summating forces in that direction. You can apply the same summation of forces from a position in which the legs are split in the sagittal plane, increasing the overloads placed on the system and the degree of difficulty. Many exercises—although specific to particular athletic skills in movement plane of limbs and involvement of certain muscle groups—are executed in a spatially exaggerated manner; that is, limbs may move through much wider ranges of motion, even though the movement plane resembles that of the performance goal.

You can accomplish a temporal overload by executing the movement as rapidly and intensely as possible. The force the skeletal muscle produces depends on the speed of shortening or lengthening and the absolute length of the muscle at any instant in time. In eccentric exercise, force increases as the velocity of stretch increases. This is in contrast to concentric exercise, in which the force decreases as the speed of the contraction increases. One theory is that the faster the transition occurs from eccentric to concentric contraction, the greater the muscular tension produced and, potentially, the greater the muscle power produced (Komi 1973). To develop in this area you can use decline pathways and springlike surfaces, as well as other variations.

Concept: We may attribute, in part, reductions in sprinting times and increases in jumping abilities, as well as other improvements in athletic performance, to training using eccentric loading and muscle elasticity (Radcliffe and Farentinos 1985).

Specificity

Another tenet of athletic training central to plyometrics is the principle of specificity. In athletic training, specificity refers to neuromuscular and metabolic adaptations of particular types of overload. Exercise stress, such as strength training for certain muscle groups, induces specific strength adaptations in particular muscular areas. For example, you can effectively achieve increases in endurance only by training for endurance. Specific exercise elicits specific adaptations, thus creating specific training effects (McArdle, Katch, and Katch 1981). If you want to jump higher or farther, you must structure your practices around jumps in those parameters. If you want speed, you must work at operating rates that are specific to those objectives. Thus, the specific plyometric or stretch-shortening cycle training effect is a methodology to develop powerful muscular responses, and you will achieve it by overloads working not only at the resistive and temporal levels but also at the spatial levels. To achieve the training effect you want from the stretch-shortening cycle requires using particular levels of resistance, speed, and space (distance covered). Overloads in the areas of resistance, timing or speed, and space or distance are important considerations. For plyometrics, you will plan a program that uses controlled frequency, intensity, duration, and specificity of training.

In the following chapters you can find a game plan of why and how to adapt, apply, and evaluate training programs involving the stretch-shortening cycle. Chapter 2 will cover preparation and chapter 3 will add tactical information. Chapters 4 and 5 give directions for basic drills. Chapter 6 will show the application of drills to specific sports and a 12-week plan for their execution. Chapter 7 discusses planning long term and evaluating your programming from the short term to the long term.

Chapter 2

Gearing Up for Plyometrics

Any program dedicated to enhancing performance needs an ongoing method of evaluating the program's direction, the participants' fitness, and the performers' accomplishments. To use the stretch-shortening cycle optimally, you should evaluate several components that you bring to the program. These include whether individuals' age, fitness level, and understanding of safe procedures are suitable for them to participate, whether they are properly equipped (having appropriate attire and props to use), and whether they can design good exercise progressions. This and the next chapter will help assure that you can conduct this evaluation.

Assessing Ability

Is serious plyometric training a good option for you? Before getting too far in planning the specifics of a program, the prudent approach is to look honestly and carefully at various factors that could affect safe participation in such intense training. If you are a trainer, you must determine a participant's status as to age, experience, health, fitness, levels of strength, and genetics. If you are planning a program for yourself, you should treat assessment at least as seriously because you are your own trainer! What you are looking for are any limitations that might inhibit proper progressive development in explosive power training.

Your Age

Chronological age is an important consideration. Carmelo Bosco and Paavo Komi (1981) conducted research to demonstrate that the maturity or immaturity of *both* the nervous system and skeletal system affect tolerance to plyometric training. Youngsters who have not yet reached puberty, for example, should not participate in plyometrics, especially at the intense levels. The continual growth of the skeletal system, cartilage at the epiphyseal plates, joint surfaces, and apophyseal insertions make the extreme forces of some plyometric exercises inappropriate.

The inability of young age groups to tolerate the high loads of the stretch-shortening cycle can cause confusion. Youngsters are exposed to forces during play and sports that may equal or exceed the forces tolerated in plyometric training with a proper progressive system. Kids are vulnerable to excessively hard play, yet not as vulnerable as to consistent repetitions of excessive overloads.

We contend that 12- to 14-year old participants can appropriately use plyometric training as preparation for future strength training. This has been corroborated by researchers including Valik (1966) and McFarlane (1982). However, we suggest moderate jump training with youths. Use early progressions of low impact and small dosages, as the guidelines in chapter 3 and the continuum in chapter 4 suggest. There does not appear to be any significant response to explosive strength training in the adolescent until after the onset of puberty; therefore, prescribe training programs cautiously. This makes using planned progressions all the more worthwhile, so individuals may receive the many other benefits (mechanics, coordination, structural integrity, etc.) until maturity and mastery develop.

As age increases, the ability of the nervous system, muscle and joint pliability, and energy production decrease, which makes plyometric training less attractive to older athletes. On the other hand, evidence suggests that a decreased explosiveness is only partly due to the natural aging process. Increases in endurance training, a lack of such training, and lifestyle also influence how much explosive power a person maintains at older ages. Continued use of stretch-shortening cycle training in proper progressions and moderate intensities can be effective for aging athletes, as evidenced by the growing numbers of masters athletes in explosive sporting events (track and field, weightlifting, etc.). As we will address in chapters 3 and 4, we can evaluate anyone's capabilities and adjust the training to accommodate both the immature and mature participant.

Your Physical Capabilities and Health Limitations

Several physical areas merit your evaluation, to assess not only for training but also for limitations. Look at *flexibility*, especially as it exists (or fails to exist) in the ankle joints and calf muscles for proper foot mechanics and in the shoulders, hips, and spine for the proper hip set and segmental cushioning. Examine *posture*, noticing especially the proper use of torso mechanics; pelvic tilt; and positioning in cervical, thoracic, and lumbar spine. Check out *balance* in equilibrium, torso tilt, and each appendage's joint alignment. Assess the *stability* of the foot as it is in contact and positioned on the ground, the firmness of stance, joint tension, and coordinated control.

Past injury may be a factor, and you must consider any that might be limiting. Look at joint stability and balance for assessing past knee, ankle, or shoulder injuries. As we will address in chapter 3, these forms of training are useful in rehabilitation from injuries. Limitations on explosive training may arise from health problems occurring in the back and spine. Excessive trauma to these or any areas that cause improper landing capabilities can present problems.

Your General Fitness

Having a good level of overall fitness is helpful in all areas of exercise, and training for explosive power is no different. Successfully completing a doctor's physical exam is helpful. You should have good body-weight control and body composition, enough cardiovascular fitness to exercise continuously for several minutes or more, the strength to handle your own body weight in movements in all planes and directions, and the flexibility to handle movement positions in several ranges of motion.

Individual Differences—Accepting Your Genes

Not all athletes will respond alike to a particular prescribed training regime. Coaches need to be sensitive to individual differences, and participants must have some self-awareness. For example, differences between males and females show up both in training and performance. In addition, the genetic makeup of an individual dictates, to a large extent, his or her ability to improve. Factors such as limb length and muscle-fiber type distribution have a direct effect on performance. You need to be aware of certain limitations that can arise in training and development. Although they may affect the rate of an athlete's progress throughout a program, they should not influence the basic design of the training regime.

Considering Experience

The training age, or level of experience, a participant brings in working with stretch-shortening cycles can be more important than chronological age. Some athletes who have had several years of experience as competitors, for example, have still never *trained* for competition. It is common to begin working with maturing athletes who have been extremely skilled in their athletic endeavors, who possess enormous talent, and yet who bring only an infantile level of training as a base. Such participants can be at high risk if they attempt to use poor technical and developmental qualities, adding quantities of exercise that their body structures are not ready for. So, as a coach, you must realistically determine a person's technical and developmental practice by quality training assessments (posture, balance, flexibility, and stability as described previously).

Judging Strength

Sport scientists have raised some interesting questions about the amount of strength and stability necessary to successfully perform eccentric training, the effects of slower isotonic strength training on eccentric performance, and whether relationships exist between more ballistic (plyometric) training and isotonic training. Traditional weight training basically enhances muscular strength. Plyometric training, on the other hand, enhances muscular *power*. Recently, Greg Wilson (1993) and others have suggested that athletes use *dynamic weight training* (a form of stretch-shortening cycle exercises that are externally loaded) to maximize mechanical output.

It is important to continually evaluate the level of strength a plyometric participant has. There are several ways to assess strength:

- Absolute strength, or the maximum level, is measured regardless of body weight.
- Relative strength, or maximum levels scaled to body weight, is important in projecting your center of gravity away from, across, or over the ground.
- Dynamic strength involves both eccentric and concentric contractions, with a degree of speed (used, for example, in squatting and single-response jumping movements).
- Elastic strength is speed involving the elastic and contractile components and reflex contractions (such as multiple response or rebound jumps).
- Core strength is discussed less often but may be the most basic and important of all.

Core strength centers on the core of the body. We will define it as the control over the muscles and joints of the trunk or torso. It is responsible for all postural stability in movements in all planes and directions. Core strength is a component of all the other forms of strength. In handling any external loads or any speed of movement, core control influences the beginning, maintenance, and completion phases (see figure 2.1).

Being able to demonstrate and assess different strength qualities (such as starting, maximal, explosive) makes an athlete more aware of the essential power qualities athletic performance demands. All forms of strength have a place in evaluation. You should prioritize them by the progressive goals and objectives of the program. For example, an athlete (Jack) may exhibit good or even great strength as tested in a barbell squat. He might be weak, however, in a vertical jump test, possibly indicating a lack of speed in the training load and poor dynamic strength. This becomes even more evident when Jack is unable to handle multiple-response movements, which indicates low levels of elastic strength. Dietmar Schmidtbleicher (1992) suggests that even different *rates* of force development are necessary to overcome differing loads, both internal and external, as well as the movement time involved.

Loading

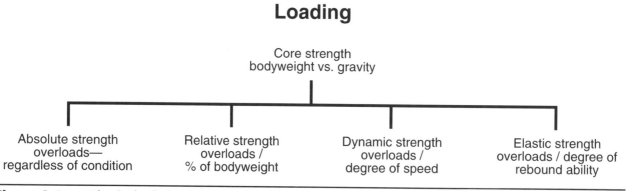

Figure 2.1   Physical adaptation to gravitational stress.

Evaluating the Exercise Objectives

You can use the stretch-shortening cycle in most parts of the training regime. It will be part of the warm-up, the weight-room workout, the speed portion, and the agility segment; sometimes you will use it specifically and others times generally.

In the quest for more efficiency in movement, minimizing the time lapse between eccentric and concentric contraction is extremely important. Two periods of delay exist. One delay is between the signal from the brain for muscle contraction and the onset of muscle activity, and the other is between that appearance of muscle electric activity and the development of tension in the muscle, the electromechanical delay (EMD). This second delay is shorter in eccentric contractions than in concentric ones. This shortened response time further supports the concept of producing the greatest force in the least amount of time. The stretch-shortening mechanism enhances force production by contributions from the series elastic component (SEC) during the stretching. Eccentric efficiency, in other words, is improved by using the stored elastic energy of the SEC.

Evaluating the factors involved with stretch-shortening cycle exercises helps determine timing, volumes, and intensities. I. King (1993) outlines these factors:

- The rate of eccentric action, known to many as the *amortization phase* (the stretch)
- The rate of concentric action, the recoil, or *summation phase* (shortening)
- The delay time between the cessation of the eccentric and onset of concentric muscle action, also known as the *coupling time*
- The amount, if any, of external load involved

These elements take only approximately one-half second to occur, yet can change the scope of the training form you are using (see figures 2.2a–2.2d). We often need to

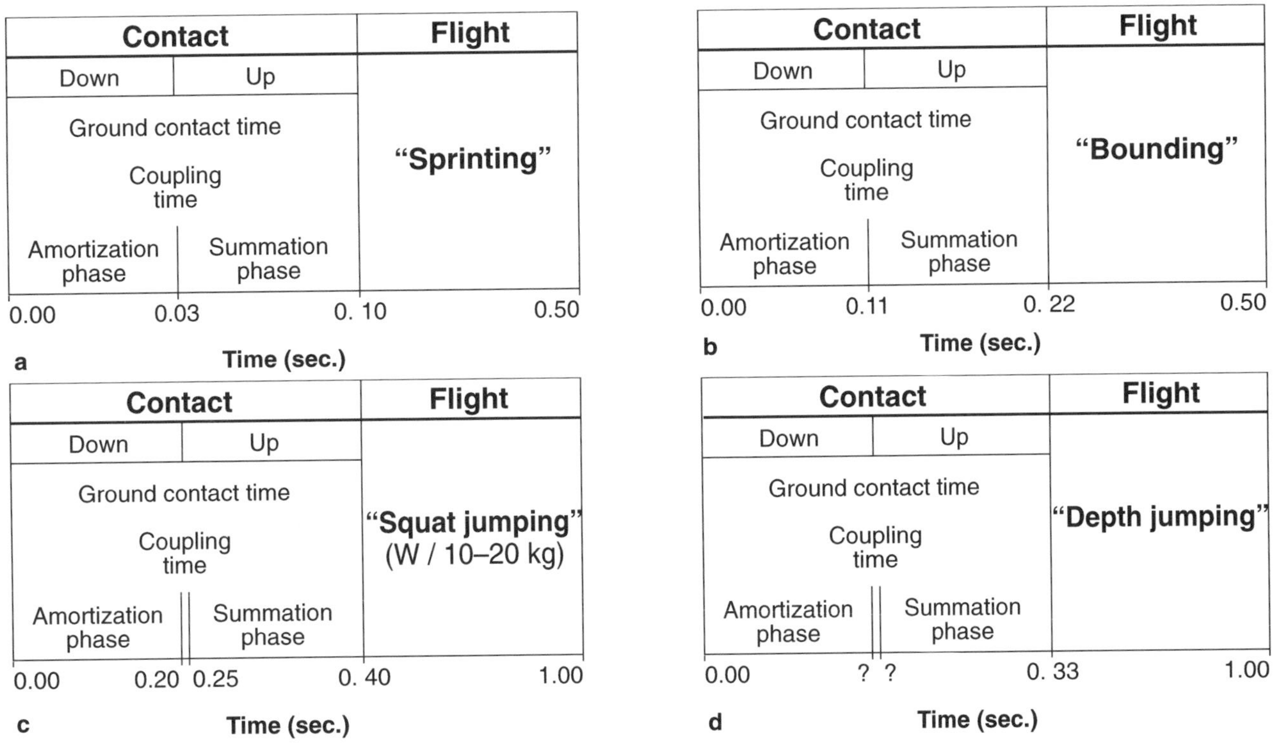

Figure 2.2 **(a)** Sprinting; **(b)** bounding; **(c)** squat jumping; **(d)** depth jumping.

distinguish a rapid continuous stretch-shortening cycle movement, or intensive elastic and reactive method, from those of a speed-strength orientation (loaded and not as elastic or reactive) or, furthermore, from a shock methodology. Schmidtbleicher (1992) considers these differences to be long or short stretch-shortening cycles—those greater or less than 250 milliseconds. In the following figures, the down portion indicates the amount of stretch, the up section shows the shortening, and the combination of the two and the delay, if any, between (coupling). These are all in the contact portions of the chart. Notice the differences in time necessary for optimally executing minimal contact time and maximal flight (see figure 2.2).

Siff and Verkhoshansky (1996) suggest that, if the coupling time is longer than about 0.15 seconds when performing drills of high impact, intensity, or rate of force development, the action is not considered classical shock-method plyometrics, such as depth jumping. For our purposes, knowing how to measure these times is not as important as understanding the differences that individual exercises make, especially when incorporating greater movement magnitudes, such as bounding versus hopping, or greater gravitational overloads, such as higher drop heights or using additional weight on the body.

As a coach, you can evaluate performance based on awareness of what ground contact or coupling time an athlete displays. You can determine the load by the response via ground contact time. It requires some theoretical understanding and observation of posture, balance, stability, and flexibility to determine what is occurring with fast movements. Because a great deal of stretch-shortening cycle improvement depends on the rate of force development and the development of neuromuscular coordination, you will need to think carefully about the style, progressive application, and specificity of plyometric exercises. For example, training using squat jumps with 15 to 20 kilograms of external weight (a sandbag or weight vest, etc.) is useful in certain phases and progressive times of training, as is bounding for certain prolonged distances. However, when training a sprinter, using this type of stretch-shortening cycle methodology doesn't attend to the specific performance needs as does lower-repetition bounding, hopping, or well-performed shock training for quicker, more impulsive repetitions of higher quality.

In considering repetitions of duration, external weight, and drops from height, it is better to wait to recommend them until an athlete is far up the skill proficiency scale. Avoid repetitions that sacrifice quality for quantity. However, you can fully use the stretch-shortening cycle throughout a continuum of exercise and load factors. Evaluating the specific goals for each training phase and the session within those phases will indicate where (along the continuum) the majority of stretch-shortening cycle volume can fall. Examples of this evaluation system are in chapter 4 (the continuum of stress and complexity).

Selecting Equipment

Performing exercises involving the stretch-shortening cycle is simple, easily located, and inexpensive. Participants can execute great plyometric training skills using backyards, parks, hallways, and even bedrooms. However, selecting the best situations for proper progressive training programs is essential to continued safe and effective training.

Facilities

When looking for a good facility or location for workouts, you will discover that Mother Nature was thinking of eccentric-style training. Grass has, in our experience, shown to be the best surface as long as it is resilient yet cushioned. We do not recommend soggy, muddy grass or dead, dry, cement-hard grass surfaces. You can use cushioned hardwood floors, such as indoor gyms and aerobic studios, for early progressions of plyometric activities, or some rugged surfaces, tarten tracks, and rubber weight-room floors. Resilient mats such as those used in gymnastic floor routines work well. Using mats with too much give or cushion defeats the purpose of reactive landings; therefore, we do not recommend anything past that of wrestling matting.

Equipment

The equipment listed here isn't costly. Some facilities have most of the listed materials. We present the following equipment list so you can decide what to select, how to select it, then how best to acquire it.

Angle Box

Made of metal, aluminum, or wood framing, an angle box is a set of angled foot placements for use in lateral movements (see figure 2.3). The precise angles of the box are not crucial. What is important is that each angle be slightly different from the other three. The bottom of the board must have enough weight, or the ability to be secured, so the box will not move during use. The boards must be of solid construction, durable, and of nonslip texture.

You can construct the angle box using the dimensions we give, or purchase similar designs through specific conditioning product catalogs.

Angle Board

The angle board is made of wood or plastic, with a metal, aluminum, or solid wood frame (see figure 2.4). The sizes of several boards differ in height and top length according to the box size you want to use. Standard sizes are a 12-inch base by 6, 8, or 10 inches in height. The boards must be of solid construction, durable, and of nonslip texture.

You can construct one using the dimensions we give, or purchase it through specific conditioning product catalogs.

Bars

Bars range in size from five feet long to seven feet long, weighing anywhere from 10 to 50 pounds. They usually measure one to two inches in diameter for Olympic style. Purchase lead pipe, steel rods, lifting bars from weight sets, or construct them from pipes, PVC, or wooden dowels.

Angle Box

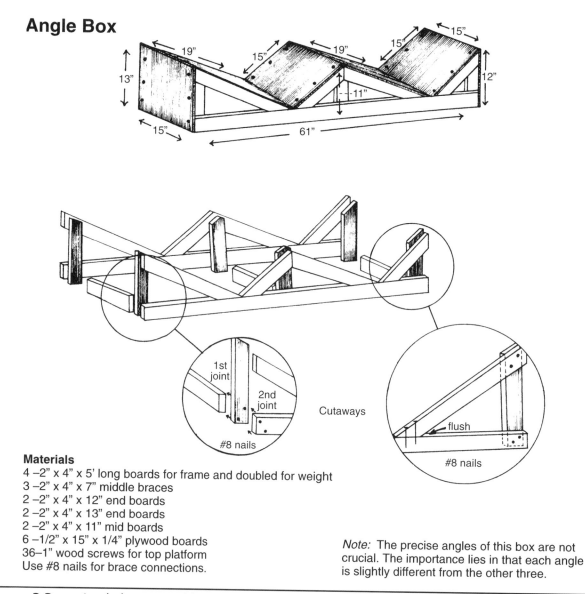

Materials
4 –2" x 4" x 5' long boards for frame and doubled for weight
3 –2" x 4" x 7" middle braces
2 –2" x 4" x 12" end boards
2 –2" x 4" x 13" end boards
2 –2" x 4" x 11" mid boards
6 –1/2" x 15" x 1/4" plywood boards
36–1" wood screws for top platform
Use #8 nails for brace connections.

Note: The precise angles of this box are not crucial. The importance lies in that each angle is slightly different from the other three.

Figure 2.3   Angle box assembly.

Boxes

Choose a variety of sizes, ranging from 12 inches high and wide to 42 inches high (see figure 2.5). You can use a combination of sizes and shapes, including rectangular and multileveled (drop, jump, and bound). Purchase boxes of wood or metal framework; you can construct boxes and cover them with rug, artificial turf, or antislip rubber.

Cones

Select rubber or plastic cones in four sizes: 6 to 8 inches, 10 to 12 inches, 16 to18 inches, and 22 to 24 inches. Buy them from sporting goods stores, catalogs (outlets), or soccer shops.

Angle Board

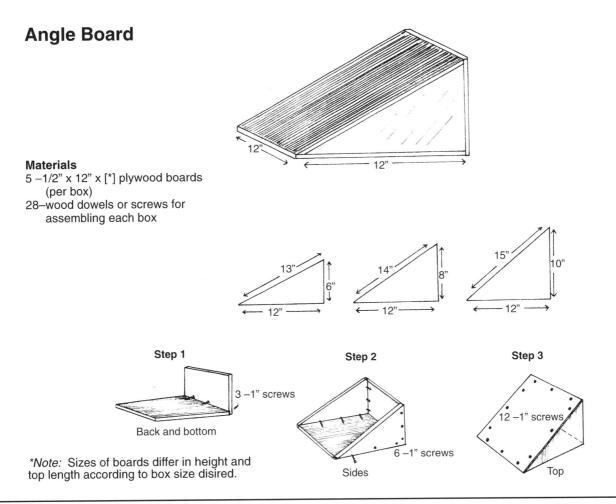

Materials
5 –1/2" x 12" x [*] plywood boards
   (per box)
28–wood dowels or screws for
   assembling each box

Step 1

3 –1" screws

Back and bottom

Note: Sizes of boards differ in height and
top length according to box size disired.

Step 2

6 –1" screws

Sides

Step 3

12 –1" screws

Top

Figure 2.4   Angle board assembly.

Dumbbells

Choose closed bells weighing 10 to 40 pounds each. They are best when solid handled. Dumbbells can be made of a solid one-piece construction, welded, or bolted. You will not use them as much for dropping as for swinging. However, some advanced methods will call for you to release the dumbbell before completion. You can buy dumbbells from any sporting goods or weight equipment outlet.

Heavy Bags

You should have a selection of heavy bags, stuffed with different combinations of foam rubber, sand, or soft pellets, and covered in canvas or durable vinyl. They can be tube or bell shaped, and they can range in weight from 20 to 120 pounds, as with many blocking dummies or boxing heavy bags. Purchase them from sporting goods outlets carrying boxing equipment or outlet catalogs of physical education equipment, football equipment, and so on. You can also construct bags with towel, shot, or sand stuffing in large laundry or carry-all bags.

Jumping Box

Materials
2 –2" x 4" x 48" boards for top
2 –2" x 4" x 16" boards for top
4 –2" x 4" x 12" studs for braces*
1 –16" x 48" x 1/4" sheet plywood
2 –12" x 48" x 1/4" sheet plywood*
2 –12" x 16" x 1/4" sheet plywood*
46-1" wood screws for attaching
    plywood boards (3 per side
    and 3-5 per side on the top)
Encase all edges and corners
with wood or aluminum molding
(light gauge). Use #8 nails for
brace connections.

Note: The height of the box can vary.
It can be 8", 12", 18", or 24".

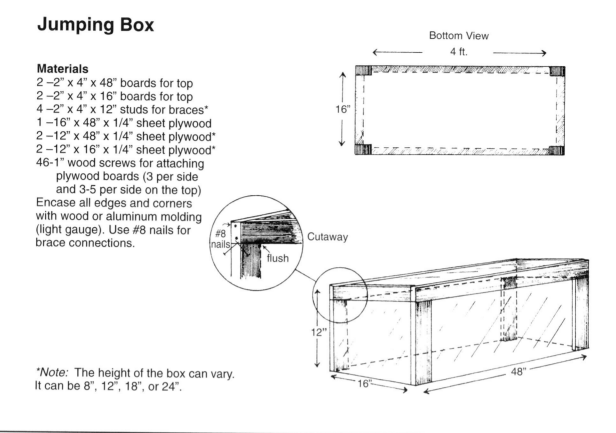

Figure 2.5   Jumping box assembly.

Hurdles

Select hurdles that are adjustable, lightweight for carrying, and a combination of aluminum, PVC, plastic, wood, or metal. You should be able to range them in height from 12 to 36 inches.

You can purchase hurdles from track and conditioning catalogs or construct them of scraps from plumbing, building, or used furniture locations.

Landing Pits

You can find landing pits outside at tracks or conditioning areas that use sand and sawdust in the dirt, or indoors, placed into or on top of ground, as landing boxes of foam padding or raised cushions.

Foam pit sizes range from 8- to 15-feet square. Sand pits can range from normal long or triple-jump pits to large ones of 5-by-30-yard rectangles.

You can purchase foam padding from sporting goods stores or outdoor and furniture repair outlets. You can get sand from rock and gravel quarries or landscaping suppliers.

Medicine Balls

Having assorted sizes of rubber or elastic balls is best, although you can use leather types if a partner aids you. The size and weight, for our purposes, range from 3 to 4 pounds, for single-limb work, to 12 to 15 pounds for total-body exercises.

It is best to purchase balls from manufacturers through a catalog or wholesale outfitter. You can also construct them from old playground or sports balls and stuff, fill, or sew them, and even wrap them in plastic or melt them in rubber.

Stair Steps

Look for stairs that are closed faced (no open space exists between steps) to prevent the toes from becoming caught underneath, no more than 6 to 8 inches high, 8 to 12 inches deep, and at least 3 feet wide.

You can find suitable steps in stadiums or indoor stairwells or can construct them of wood or cement.

Tubing or Bands

You can use elastic tubing to assist with accelerated movements or to provide safe obstacles for incremental jumping. Select assorted sizes and dimensions of surgical cord to solid core rubber cord. We recommend the thicker, more solid styles. Dimensions range from one-eighth-inch to three-quarter-inch thicknesses (inquire whether that is the total diameter or the width of the tubing wall). Size ranges may come in light, medium, and heavy specifications also, as with some wider styles of rubber bands.

You can purchase tubes and bands at hospital or pharmaceutical supply outlets, catalogs, or conditioning product catalogs.

Attire

There isn't any special attire necessary for explosive power training. Any athletic workout clothing that is comfortable; wears well; and does not bind, hinder, or confine the joint movements is acceptable.

Shoes

Shoes have been given much importance regarding explosive training. The comfort, stability, and design of the shoe does play a part, especially with continued and constant training. However, the main issue is proper foot, ankle, and lower leg-landing positions (see chapter 3). These mechanics should be the most important emphasis. Experience and clinical evidence indicate that barefoot or thin-soled footwear may be safe and reliable from the standpoint of decreased tendency for pronation, minimizing excessive heel contact, and other landing improprieties. The proper blend of exercise surface and footwear that fosters attention to mechanics is what we should strive for.

Weighted Apparel

All styles of weighted apparel (vests, belts, anklets, etc.) have undergone clinical and practical evaluation, many with successful results. We do not recommend prolonged use of any particular style and advise against any use in the progressive beginning and intermediate areas of programming.

Once in the advanced stages of training, base your use of weighted apparel on what will produce the best results for optimal hip projection. Use any piece that exhibits the best fit, contour, and efficiency of use and does not detract from the ultimate goals of hip projection and proprioceptive augmentation. You can purchase suitable attire in many sporting goods outlets and conditioning equipment catalogs.

Chapter 3

Plyometrics Technique

In training with plyometric exercises, just as with other forms of stretch-shortening cycle or athletic training, it is important to follow certain guidelines to ensure safety as well as proper and effective performance. In this chapter we emphasize basic aspects of training that are the keys to good technique.

Warm-Up and Cool-Down

Because plyometric exercises emphasize posture, balance, flexibility, stability, and mobility, you should precede all drills with an adequate warm-up and conclude with a proper cooldown. Preparatory warm-up routines include jogging, calisthenics, and dynamic stretching methods, which are important to ensure the musculoskeletal systems are activated and prepared (see table 3.1). Static stretching can follow to ensure well-loosened muscles connecting all the joints and tendons you will use in subsequent activity.

After the general warm-up, doing specific warm-up routines will ensure optimal preparation for quality work (see table 3.1). We also emphasize technical form running (forward, lateral, and backward), lifting (using a light bar or stick in pulling, squatting, and pushing movements), and progressive takeoff and throwing motions, and we will explain these in later chapters.

Table 3.1	**Warm-Up and Cooldown Activity**

Preparatory Warm-up

General

Walking (heel to buttocks, knee to chest, marching)
Lunging (forward, side to side, and backward)
Crawling (hands on the ground and heels on the ground)
Jogging (smooth, relaxed, easy gait, shortened strides of 1/4 speed)
Skipping (stepping and hopping, with exaggerated swinging of the arms)
Shuffling (side to side glide without crossing the feet and exaggerated arm swings)
Carioka (grapevine movement of step, step behind, step, step in front twisting the hips)
Backward run (tall, relaxed, long easy strides that reach back)
Stationary bike (low progressions of speed and intensity)
Treadmill (simple and short progressions of light intensity)
Slideboard (lateral skating movements of short duration)
Rope skipping (short durations of simple one- and two-foot combinations)

Dynamic flexibility	**Static/active stretch**
Neck rotations	Shoulders and arms
Shoulder rolls (arms hang)	Back
Shoulder rotations (arms involved)	Hips
Trunk twist	Hamstrings
Hip rotations	Groin
Knee rolls	Quadriceps
Ankle rotations	Calves
Leg swings (long, bent, and side to side)	

Technical Form Running and Lifting

Forward

Mach drills (walk, skip, run routines of "A" acceleration and "B" speed mechanics)
• Fast skip (emphasis on push and dynamic leg and hip mechanics)
• Slide kick (emphasis on high heel recovery upward rather than backward)
• Rhythm and cadence (interval combinations of sprint and stride mechanics with one leg)
• Fast leg cadence (continuous sprint and stride combinations one leg at a time)

Lateral

Shuffle (side to side step routine of long efficient strides and a low hip posture)
Slides (side to side glide routine of short strides for quick change of direction)
Lateral skip (side to side step-hop routine with a low hip posture)
Carioka (hip twisting strides of alternating steps in front then behind)
Crossover run (segmental lower body forward running as the upper torso faces sideways)

| Table 3.1 | Warm-Up and Cooldown Activity *(continued)* |

Backward

Backward run (mimicking forward running posture while moving backwards)
Backpedal (maintaining a low hip posture, short strides that remain underneath the torso)
Backward skip (backpedal posture with a step-hop foot cadence)
Backward shuffle (shuffle steps back with pivots, while facing forward continuously)
Backward kick-slide (a galloping effect of back leg kick and reach with foreleg push)

Pulling	**Pushing**	**Squatting**
Good morning	Behind-neck press	Overhead squat
Stiff-leg deadlift	Military press(front)	Overhead lunge
Bar twist (slow)	Alternating press	45-degree or side lunge

Cooldown (recovery and restoration)

Stretching	**Hydrotherapy**	**Nutrition**
Jog/stride/cycle	Hot and cold shower massage	Fluid replacement
Active isolation	Cool tub/pool work	Carbohydrate
Contract-relax/passive	Ice bath	consumption

It is important that the sessions menu be short but intense. The design of the training session must adhere to an efficient pattern of timely execution to preserve the warmth of the musculoskeletal systems and maintain their energy.

After the warm-up, you must maintain core warmth, which is not mere external sweating or feeling the warmth of the environment. Here's a good example: An athlete spends the proper amount of time warming up, then makes his first activity a lying- or sitting-down exercise (e.g., bench press). After 10 to 15 minutes of this, he decides to do some squatting, pulling, or jumping exercise. He still feels warm and is perspiring, but the body at its core has been lying down for all that time, even if he was pushing or moving with intensity. This is an example of poor session design because, though he feels warm, his core muscular condition went down. Even though he got back to pulling and squatting and still feels warm, this condition is more external than internal (spinal and pelvic). See our "workout creeds" below for a good example of session management with emphasis on explosive power.

Notice that table 3.1 shows a third element, cooling down. Perform the cooldown as the final portion of the workout session, in a relaxed, yet productive and efficient manner. This is to ensure that you have begun adequate recovery and restoration. Our workouts follow a belief that six basic elements make a good session: warming up, dynamic work, strength work with multiple-joint movements, isolated work, mobility work, and cooling down to begin restoration.

Workout Creeds

1. **Warm-up**
   - General (jog, skip, crawl, stretch, etc.)
   - Core (abdominal, low back)
   - Specific (technique work)

2. **Dynamic Work**
   - Explosive movements (snatches, jumps, throws, starts, etc.)

3. **Strength Work**
   - Heavy multiple joint movements (squats, jerks, loaded sprints, etc.)

4. **Isolated Work**
   - Lying or seated movements (bench, pulleys, etc.)

5. **Mobility Work**
   - Fluid, full body movements (agilities, stretching, recovery strides, etc.)

6. **Cooldown**

Building a Foundation

Before getting into a progressive 12-week program, you should assure that a participant has a proper foundation. This involves a general level of strength, continual testing to be able to select appropriate exercises, exercising with good fundamental techniques, avoiding risks of injury, and knowing how to recuperate from workouts.

Strength Training

Because a strength base is advantageous in plyometric and stretch-shortening cycle training, you should design a general strength-training program to complement, not retard, the development of explosive power. However, you don't have to overdo establishing a strength base before plyometric training. An often prescribed recommendation in much of the layman's literature is the once-used Russian suggestion of a maximum squat of 1.5 to 2 times the body's weight before attempting depth jumps and similar shock training. This criterion is still useful as a safety protocol for the extreme end of the stress continuum. However, you do not need to apply it to the successful performance and positive training effects of the other stretch-shortening cycle exercises that fall along the progressive criterion. In our more recent research (Radcliffe and Osternig 1995), we found that some trends exist between squat performance and depth-jump capabilities. However, the significance was so low that any predictions about how well amount of weight squatted determined jump stress capabilities are negligible.

Ongoing Assessments

Begin all progressions with testing the posture, balance, stability, and flexibility of each participant before you perform any training. Examples of simple evaluation indexes would be performing a body-weight squat with erect torso, through hip and knee flexion, full-foot contact with balance over the midfoot, and relative strength throughout the movement (see figure 3.1). Vern Gambetta's research (1989) suggests that for beginners, strength in the stabilizing muscles is primary, and you can easily test for it. The advantage of assessing posture, balance, stability, and flexibility is that you will have information to guide your planning for progression to the next training level on the continuum. These assessments are useful for all stretch-shortening cycle training movements (weights, plyometrics, speed and agility work, etc.). If progress in any area seems doubtful to you, drop back a level or maintain the current level until you meet the criteria. Then you can move onward.

Figure 3.1

Vertical Jump Test

Countermovement vertical jump height has been used as a test protocol to measure successful depth-jump performance. Researchers have used several practical testing conventions in this area. As long ago as 1974, Sergio Zanon suggested a protocol:

> *An athlete is made to carry out a standing high jump after flexing his legs and the maximum height is reached with his hand on a graduated board (vertical jump test). The highest reading of three jumps is registered. The athlete is made to carry out the same operation, landing on the same point from a height which is progressively higher by 20-40-60 cms. (depth jump test), and from each different height of fall, the maximum height is reached and the subsequent jump is read off of the graduated board. . . . The value of the greater height reached in the subsequent jump (after landing) which should always be higher than that of the jump from level '0' (standing jump) determines the optimum height of fall for that particular athlete at that moment of the training process.*

Practical field work by Frank Costello (1984) supported this concept. He suggested that, by knowing an athlete's sergeant (standard) vertical jump, then testing in a depth jump from an 18-inch box, relatively weak athletes will jump several inches less than their vertical jump marks, as opposed to stronger athletes who will reach or exceed their vertical jump marks after a drop from the same height.

Other Basic Tests

In chapter 7 we will describe a basic testing procedure that we have identified and believe is helpful in evaluating power. It involves these tests:

1. Standing-landing jump tests
2. Vertical jump
3. Depth jump
4. Medicine ball chest pass
5. Medicine ball overhead throw forward
6. Medicine ball overhead throw backward
7. Jumps decathlon

You can also find normative data and ranked improvement progressions in chapter 7 as a way to interpret test scores and individualize training programs. Testing at the beginning of certain training phases, then retesting at the conclusion of a training phase allows you to evaluate whether the intensity and dosage of the training are correct, too little, or too much. By conferring with the athletes and evaluating the intensity and volumes of the workload, you can systematically monitor the progress and develop a better basis for making adjustments in training. If you keep records and share normative data, as we have done in this book, we can collectively develop better prescriptions for training.

Remember the Basics

Whether you are the participant reading this book or a coach who will guide others, you should keep in mind several components of the stretch-shortening cycle and plyometric training principles as you evaluate your teaching, learning, and testing: You want to teach others basic progressions and assessment procedures that provide good training and lead to more complex training methodologies.

Remind athletes of these rules:

- The toe-up rule, which is using locked ankles in dorsiflexion, with full mid- to forefoot ground contact upon landing
- The knee-up and hip-up rules, which promote maximum knee drive and hip extension or projection
- The heel-up rule for further projection of the hips and body flight by reducing the arc and rate of the swing leg
- The thumbs-up or blocking rule for upper body posture and continued force expression

Applying these rules in an accelerated manner during support leg coupling is known as transference of force (Jacoby and Fraley 1995).

Use sensible progressions in your teaching and working out. Here are a few guidelines:

- Teach exercise execution centered first around the lower leg (pogo, galloping, prancing, and ankle flip).
- Progress from lower-leg to full-leg countermovements (squat jump, split jump, and single-leg stair bound).
- Finally, progress to total torso countermovements (knee-tuck jump, bounding, hopping, etc.).

• With medicine balls, the execution should be passing, tossing, then throwing movements; next do the full multiple recoil movements of thrusting, swinging, and repetitive throws.

Educate athletes about relaxation, especially of the face and neck, to optimally perform with postural control. Using proper breathing mechanics is crucial and can assist in structural support and execution:

• Inhale during descent.
• Hold breath during stretch phase.
• Exhale once you have executed shortening.

Teach, learn, coach, and train progressively along the stress continuum (see details in chapters 4 and 6).

Landings

As mentioned in chapter 1, specificity training in plyometrics is as important as in strength and endurance training. Generally, you should perform plyometric exercises at amplitudes and intensities corresponding closely to the power movements and action sequences of specific sport skills. Sometimes, however, it's useful to include purposeful temporal and spatial exaggerations as overload mechanisms.

Performing jumps with undamped (without delay) landings produces higher power and force values than those with damped landings (landings with added flexion, therefore more delay in coupling and contact times). The quicker the person switches from yielding work to overcoming work, the more powerful, and safer, the response.

In most cases, a good guideline to follow is that athletes should execute undamped landings in jumping exercises. All progressions and advancement in stretch-shortening cycle exercise execution should stress active tension upon landings. Both clinical and practical evidence exists about conditioning the participants in the art of preparing the musculature for takeoffs upon landing. In an effort to minimize ground time and promote undamped, high-tension, optimum-impulse takeoffs, you want to flex the joints and tense the stretch components upon landing, rather than after contact with the ground (Bosco 1982).

Foot Placement

Proper foot placement when doing the yielding and overcoming work is essential. To obtain as quick a release as possible, an athlete must maintain a locked ankle when landing on the ground. Rolling the foot from heel to toe or allowing movement along the ankle joint slows the response and displaces the force away from the overcoming portion. The best way to land on the ground is with a dorsiflexed foot and two-thirds to full-foot ground contact upon landing, emphasizing that the weight be balanced on the front half of the foot.

If you emphasize landing on the toes or even on the ball of the foot, an athlete might become confused, leading to poorly balanced landings and inadequate specificity in most leg and foot movements involving acceleration. As drills and execution techniques progress, the ability to reaccelerate the leg and paw the foot to grab the ground will be available, giving the optimal use of the least amount of ground-contact time.

Blocking or Thumbs-Up Rule

In all plyometric jumps, hops, leaps, bounds, skips, and ricochets, concentrate on the blocking (thumbs-up) rule, by adding the arms in a forward and upward punching motion. The block occurs by abruptly halting the motion, to maintain upper-body posture and continue force expression. When you bring the knees upward abruptly, as in hopping and tucking movements, the tendency is for the shoulders to drop forward. Holding the hands in thumbs-up position and executing the block technique counteracts this tendency by forcing the torso to remain more upright, thus aiding balance. In addition, the blocking motion of the upper torso can provide some 10 to 12 percent of the forces you apply.

Follow-Through

Follow-through is important in plyometric movements involving upper-body muscle groups. You should apply force continuously and emphasize quickness of action. In repetitive throws, such as the medicine ball chest pass or the heavy bag thrust, try to prevent the recovery or catch phase from going beyond the point of full extension or flexion. This will ensure that limb and trunk musculature is properly stretched (loaded), initiating a more forceful, reactive explosion.

Dilemmas of Eccentric Exercise

Eccentric exercise has been shown to produce damage in muscle cells and in motor performance. High-force eccentric exercise places considerable stress on muscle and connective tissue. It tends to produce delayed-onset muscle soreness. However, various sport scientists (including Fritz and Stauber 1988; Frid'en 1984; Ebbeling and Clarkson 1990) have found data suggesting that damaged connective tissue and muscle relates to important regeneration processes. The eccentric side of contraction also seems to cause increased intramuscular fluid pressure as a factor associated with delayed muscle soreness. This is significant for plyometric participants; some of this damage has a positive side connected with the regeneration process. It is helpful to understand these concepts to be able to better assess training, fatigue, overuse, and recovery.

Eccentric contractions cause more changes in certain muscle functions than do concentric contractions. These changes seem to be the result of trauma, initially in the mechanics. However, with time chemical changes also occur, due to the high tensions generated during eccentric loading. This type of loading has also been associated with some occurrence of tendinitis. Greater forces during eccentric contractions, according to Curwin and Stanish (1984), create greater stress on the tendons of the involved joints. Evidence of damage to the tendon microstructures seems to be the major factor involved.

The increased use of eccentric muscular exercise to augment performance and rehabilitation has generated questions about optimal and safe training loads. For practitioners, a great concern is that there is no consensus about what constitutes appropriate volumes and intensities of the stretch-shortening cycle or eccentric loading exercises. The type, duration, intensity, and dosage of elastic and stretch-shortening cycle training protocols needs continuous evaluation. Developments over the last 15 years, by study and by practical evaluation, have helped us greatly in dosage recommendations. This is another reason the progression tables in later chapters can be so valuable.

Eccentric action deserves special consideration from the physiological, adaptive, and training standpoints, because eccentric muscle contraction can absorb shock, a function different from other muscle actions. Training using only eccentric actions eliminates the inhibitory actions allowing for improvement in muscle strength and function. This shows us a further need for examining the balance of eccentric and concentric muscle regimen and understanding the optimal use of eccentric and stretch-shortening cycle training methodologies (Stauber 1989).

Therefore, continued damage to myofibers or connective tissue and continued repair and adaptation are long-term training effects of repeated eccentric muscle actions. Recovery from this form of exercise tends to be a slow process. Complete recovery can possibly take a week to 10 days, especially when an athlete does unaccustomed eccentric work. On the other hand, repeated bouts of eccentric exercise can produce adaptation, before complete recovery and restoration. Repeated, long-term eccentric tensions reorganize and recoordinate muscle fiber structures, resulting in better stretchability and reduced mechanical damage. A fine line can exist in results from heavy exercise bouts with eccentric contractions: injury or microtearing of muscle fiber compared with helpful adaptations that improve power and plyometric overloads that can become harmful compared with those that produce great results due to adaptation. The common denominator is the work-to-rest ratio, and we will explain this with more detail later in the chapter.

We should now consider eccentric loading along with prestretch exercises and prelanding postures. A major factor in treating (or rehabilitating) eccentric loading problems is initiating force-reducing techniques in the execution of eccentric training along with treatment. This means that it is important to use prestretch exercises for the agonistic muscles to maintain good mechanics and use postural control during eccentric movements. The subsequent effects of a premotion silent period, a possible central-motor control system to stretch the agonist while reinforcing the dynamic forces that follow, seems to significantly reduce the forces in dynamic and ballistic movements (Aoki, Tsukahara, and Yabe 1989). Just as we will do in the different training phases of the stretch-shortening cycle, we can progress through rehabilitative phases using the same concepts.

In rehabilitative terms, this means slow, controlled, eccentric movements, developing to the point at which you can control much higher velocities with eccentric, contractile stopping abilities. Let's take jumping in stretch-shortening cycle training, for instance. Landing technique is the primary issue. How well you land will dictate how well you next take off. By executing the proper prelanding posture and give with the landing impact, the impulsive reversal of motion becomes the ultimate feature of the training.

Beginners should start with moderate drills, such as in-place jumps, and drills with both legs. As you see strength and explosive power increase, you can progress to movement drills and increasing intensity and complexity.

Progressive Overload

A plyometric training program must provide resistive, spatial, and temporal overload. Overload forces the neuromuscular system to work at greater intensities. You regulate proper overload by controlling the height, distance, external loads or forces (or both), and the dosage (volume of work) of each variable. Improper overload may negate the effectiveness of the exercise or may even result in injury. Thus, using weights that exceed the resistive overload demands of certain plyometric movements may increase strength but not necessarily explosive power. Resistive overload in most plyometric exercises takes the form of forces of momentum and gravity, using light-weight objects such as medicine balls or dumbbells, or merely body weight. Later in this chapter we will deal more comprehensively with this concept.

Volume and Dosage

Usually the number of sets and repetitions coincides with the type, complexity, and intensity of the exercises involving stretch-shortening cycle training. The amount should also reflect the planning stages, the progressions, and levels of development that you have achieved. Usually the number of repetitions ranges from 8 to 12, with fewer repetitions for more complex takeoff and landing sequences and more repetitions for those exercises with lower stress. The number of sets may vary accordingly. Sport scientists in eastern Europe have suggested 6 to 10 sets for most exercises; whereas earlier Russian sport scientists recommended from 3 to 6 sets, especially for the more intense jumping drills. We emphasize that you plan all dosages on the continuum of progressive development as dictated by stress and exercise complexity (see figure 3.2).

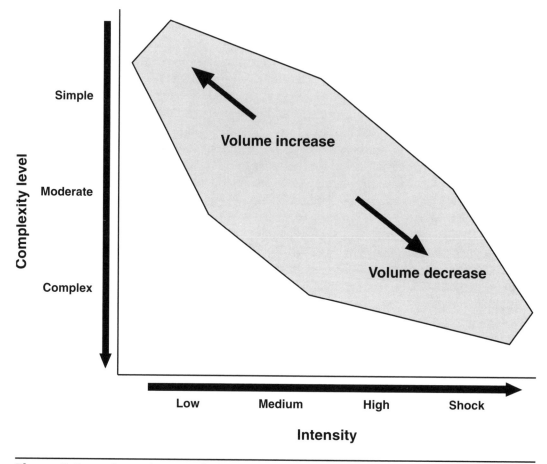

Figure 3.2   A continuum of progressive development.

In the 1970s Russian scientists Verkhoshansky and Tatyan (1973) showed that, with high-volume speed-strength training, the sequencing of speed-strength training for preparing athletes is not statistically significant. This type of training is most effective when simultaneously used speed-strength preparation coordinates with the current functional state of the athlete's body. Sometimes the number of repetitions is dictated not only by the intensity of the drill but also by the athlete's condition, the execution of each repetition, and the value of the outcome.

Single- and Multiple-Response Drills

Most stretch-shortening cycle drills fall into one of two categories: single-response (SR) or multiple-response (MR) drills. The single-response drills represent a single, intense effort. Good examples are takeoffs, initial bursts of motion, and releases. Multiple-response drills, though also intense, place more emphasis on elasticity, speed, and coordination by involving several efforts in succession. One major goal of true plyometric training is accomplishing high-impulse landings and takeoffs in succession. To properly progress to the advanced stages of the stretch-shortening cycle and plyometric training continuum, you must use both types of response. Even better, you should insert a third, which we call multiple response with a pause, working it into the educational setting of the training.

In the teaching and learning progressions, perform single-response drills with a complete self-check and reset of the posture, balance, stability, and flexibility at each takeoff and landing. Successful performance then leads to executing the exercise in a single-response manner without resetting: takeoff, land, pause and check, then repeat. Therefore, because of the no-reset factor, the drill becomes a continued set of responses, but with pauses. Continued success will lead to multiple-response repetitions and progressions.

You are performing these drills to improve nerve-muscle reactions, explosiveness, quickness, and the ability to generate forces in certain directions. An athlete will only benefit from the number of repetitions done well. For example, if he or she performs a set of hops, bounds, or throws correctly for eight repetitions, but begins to fatigue and performs incorrectly thereafter, then eight repetitions is enough. In the elastic-reactive nature of this training, little is gained with low effort, poorly executed exercises. Several coaches and researchers have used high-volume drills and exercises to investigate the effectiveness of high-endurance elasticity, but the nature of the exercises is low impact and intensity, and low movement complexity. Referring to the basic progression guidelines section of this chapter, we see that training effects occur with quality before quantity.

The number of sets, repetitions, and rest periods we recommend in the following chapters are based on our experiences of teaching and coaching plyometric training at the junior high, high school, collegiate, professional, and elite athlete levels, and on research literature for particular drills. They are not absolutes, but merely a basis from which you can begin, then evaluate, and progress. Adjust the values within the objectives to achieve the optimal training goals. Volume of plyometric training is an inexact science at this time, and we need much further research in this area.

High Intensity

We can describe intensity two ways, both important to stretch-shortening cycle training. One description deals with the amount of force at impact. We will address this in more detail later. The other use of the term deals with the level of effort while executing the drills. Once you have implemented warm-up and progressive lead-up exercises, quickness of execution with maximal effort is essential for optimal training effects. The rate of muscle stretch is more important than the magnitude of the stretch. You achieve a greater reflex response when you load the muscle rapidly. Regardless of the level of progression, you must expend maximum effort projecting the hips, torso, appendages, or implement. Reducing impact, complexity, or flight is dictated by the technique and constraints of the exercise progressions themselves, not by diminished effort. Because you must perform the exercises intensely, it is important to rest adequately between successive exercise sequences.

Maximize Force and Minimize Time

Both force and velocity of movement are important in plyometric training. In many cases the critical concern is the speed at which you can perform a particular action. For example, in shot putting the primary objective is to exert maximum force throughout the putting movement. The quicker you execute the action sequence, the greater the force you will generate and the longer the distance you will achieve. As we defined it in chapter 1, the impulse of the movement is key. Movements must have a high impulse to genuinely train in the manner that the stretch-shortening cycle and plyometrics have suggested. The measure of impulsive action may truly dictate the effectiveness of training and performance.

Rest

A rest period of one or two minutes between sets is usually sufficient for the neuromuscular systems stressed by stretch-shortening cycle exercises to recuperate. Much depends on where the exercises exist along the stress scale. Exercises of low impact and landing or catching intensity (medicine ball, heavy bag) may allow minimal rest periods of 30 to 60 seconds, enough time to walk back or change places with a partner or group of practitioners. At the shock end of the stress scale, exercise repetitions may require 2+ to 3 minutes or more for the systems to be available to produce, and handle, the forces necessary for optimal execution. An adequate period of rest between training days is important for proper recovery of muscles, ligaments, and tendons.

The frequency most trainers advocate is two or three days per week of plyometric training, which seems to give optimal results. It is important to consider the total training load, the type of activity in the sport's specificity, and the influence of the inverse relationship between frequency and intensity.

Noted authorities (Gambetta et al. 1986) suggest that you use the emphasis of the training day as the major guideline when planning the workouts. When you do plyometric activities on the same days as other lifting, sprinting, or throwing activities, prioritize their importance. If the goal is the elastic strength effects, then make the volume of plyometric work larger and place it earlier in the workout day—before more relative or dynamic strength work. If the elastic effects have lower priority than other speed or strength work, then the plyometric work may follow those workout activities and you can adjust their dosages accordingly. In addition, within the training microcycle (week), attention to different strength modalities coexists (e.g., dynamic versus absolute), which can also dictate where you need to place elastic strength work. Table 3.2 gives examples of workout weeks that are successful for programs with a restricted time system.

Table 3.2   **Weekly Workout Schedule**

Sunday	Monday	Tuesday	Wednesday	Thursday	Friday	Saturday
Rest	Warm-up Technique Strength Speed endurance Cooldown	Warm-up Technique Elastic Speed Cooldown	Warm-up Technique Strength Cooldown	Warm-up Technique Elastic Speed Cooldown	Warm-up Technique Strength Speed endurance Cooldown	Active rest
Rest	Warm-up Technique Strength Speed Elastic Cooldown	Warm-up Technique Strength Cooldown	Warm-up Speed endurance Cooldown	Warm-up Technique Strength Speed Elastic Cooldown	Warm-up Technique Strength Cooldown	Active rest
Rest	Warm-up Technique Strength Speed endurance Cooldown	Warm-up Technique Speed Elastic Cooldown	Warm-up Technique Strength Cooldown	Active rest	Warm-up Technique Elastic Strength Speed Cooldown	Warm-up Technique Speed endurance Cooldown
Warm-up Technique Speed endurance Cooldown	Warm-up Technique Elastic Strength Speed Cooldown	Active rest	Warm-up Technique Strength Cooldown	Warm-up Technique Speed Elastic Cooldown	Warm-up Technique Strength Speed endurance Cooldown	Rest
Competitive Phase						
Rest	Warm-up Technique Elastic Strength Cooldown	Warm-up Technique Speed Cooldown	Warm-up Technique Strength Elastic Cooldown	Warm-up Technique Strength Speed Cooldown	Warm-up Technique Special Cooldown	Competition day
Rest	Warm-up Technique Strength Speed endurance Cooldown	Warm-up Technique Speed Elastic Cooldown	Warm-up Technique Speed Strength Cooldown	Warm-up Technique Special Cooldown	Competition day	Warm-up Technique Strength Cooldown

Complex Training

On some combined strength and elastic work days, an efficient method of time and facility use is strength, speed, and elastic *complexes*. Our definition of a complex is when the sets of two different exercise styles follow one another, unlike *combinations*, which we define as the repetitions of two different exercise styles following one another. For example, we consider a set of three repetitions of clean and jerk a combination (clean and jerk). An athlete performs one clean repetition, followed by the jerk repetition, then repeats this sequence two more times. Had the athlete completed all three clean repetitions, then started the execution of the three jerk repetitions, this would be a complex (clean then jerk) exercise.

Complex training methods can also involve attaching two exercises that are similar in movement pattern and fall into the different labels of absolute or relative strength (speed not a factor), and those of elastic (speed and rebound ability). For further definition of these strength terms refer to chapter 2. Examples of complexes of absolute strength and elastic strength (weights and plyometrics) that have been successful for us are squatting then jumping, pressing then passing, pulling then tossing or throwing, and lunging then bounding or skipping.

- Barbell back squat then squat jump 5 × 4—do a set of 5 repetitions of barbell back squat, followed immediately by a set of 4 squat jumps, then rest. Increase the weight of the barbell; then repeat the sequence for 3 more sets. You may perform the squat jumps with a light weight (25-pound sandbag, etc.) eventually. In the beginning use only body weight.

- Incline press or bench press then medicine ball chest pass (for height) 5 × 5—begin with a set of 5 repetitions of incline press, followed immediately by 5 repetitions of medicine ball chest pass with a 7- to 15-pound medicine ball, then rest. Increase the amount of weight on the barbell if necessary to intensify those repetitions, and repeat the sequence. The medicine ball weight does not increase.

Individualizing the Training Program

For best results, you will want to individualize the plyometric training program. After you have evaluated the participant, trained him or her in the basics, and observed some exercises, you should have a good idea of what each athlete is capable of doing and how fast to progress. Despite continuing research in the area of optimal training loads, as with so many other areas of sport training, individualizing the stretch-shortening cycle training program is more of an art than a science.

The intensity and amount of overload are two critical variables here. Views vary about the optimum intensity and overload for different stretch-shortening cycle exercises. Many coaches still recommend that athletes be able to squat 1+ to 2 times their body weight, for example, to train with certain plyometric exercises. However, as we mentioned previously, this does not apply to all exercises under the stress continuum of the stretch-shortening cycle, nor is it appropriate for every individual.

As we will discuss later, simple tests of progression and evaluation can provide a basis for individualizing the training, even if these tests are not yet based on a substantial body of scientific research evidence.

One notable area in which there is good evidence is the depth-jump exercise. Bosco and Komi (1979, 1981) and Verkhoshansky (1967) examined the optimal height for executing depth jumps and found that dropping from a height of 29 inches develops speed. They found, in contrast, that dropping from 43 inches develops dynamic strength. Higher than 43 inches, the time and energy it takes to cushion the force of the drop to the ground defeats the purpose for this shock training.

More than three decades ago, Verkhoshansky first addressed the usefulness of depth jumps as an eccentric loading exercise. He searched for a shock method of nerve-muscle reactive ability in a takeoff after jumping from a height. He demonstrated that isotonic weight training marginally improved speed of running and jumping takeoff. Verkhoshansky stated that "jumps in-depth come the closest to bridging the gap between weight or strength training and jump training for speed," adding, "Takeoffs after a jump for depth was the leading method of improving the reactive ability of the nerve-muscle apparatus" (Verkhoshansky 1968).

Bosco and Komi (1982) reported improvements in jumping ability and increased tolerance to stretch loads in what they termed bounce training (drop jumps). After studying an athlete's behavior under impact (depth jumps), Bobbert and others (Bobbert et al. 1986; Bobbert, Huijing, and van Ingen Schenau 1987a, b), who also analyzed techniques of drop and countermovement jumps (and the force of their impact), recommended choosing drop heights that do not require heel-to-ground contact. Athletes should land with the weight distributed toward the forward half of the feet, because landing on a flat foot may excessively strain the Achilles tendon.

When eccentric training was introduced in the 1960s, it was assumed that high drop jumps (75-115 centimeters or 30-45 inches) were necessary to achieve maximum results (Verkhoshansky 1968). Later, studies recommended that drop heights should not exceed 40 to 60 centimeters or 16 to 24 inches (Komi and Bosco 1978; Scoles 1978; Viitasalo and Bosco 1982; Clutch et al. 1983; Bosco and Komi 1979, 1982; Adams 1984; Hakkinen, Alen, and Komi 1985). Our studies (Radcliffe and Osternig 1995) and others (Bobbert et al. 1986; Bobbert, Huijing, and van Ingen Schenau 1987a, b) indicate that a further reduction in drop height may be appropriate (20 to 40 centimeters or 8 to 16 inches).

Specificity

As we mentioned in the first chapter, improving performance requires using the principle of specific training and development. The dynamic structures of a skill are located in the muscular components of force, contraction, and recruitment. Training concepts in a spatial orientation can help this development, for example, using positions that mimic the same angles and degrees of contraction, improving neuromuscular skills, and showing measurable increases in performance. These increases become evident when, whether simple or complex, the movements you train are the same movements you evaluate in testing. The principles that put the body's postures into their movement planes include the patterns, regions, frequencies, and velocities of the performance movements (Bompa 1993; Siff 1996).

When you train for specific strength, speed, and endurance, keep in mind that stretch-shortening cycle exercises are useful for a variety of the phases and elements of the overload, intensity, and dosage principles. Different phases of training require various preparatory, technical, developmental, and transitional methods. Using different progressive levels of stretch-shortening cycle training, you can train the general, multilateral, and specific aspects as you phase them in and out of the training development. Training age, rehabilitation, and closeness of a competitive performance each should influence the timing and dosages of specific plyometric movements.

We recommend that you continue using the progressive exercise methods to develop the general processes of strength (for example, the relative and dynamic portions) while you move to more reactive portions with shock methodology as in the advanced stages. The progressions are necessary to continue fostering greater neuromotor (proprioceptive) development. Then, with complete knowledge of your sport or activity, apply the stretch-shortening cycle principles to developing highly specific, neuromuscular improvements in performance parameters.

Training and Rehabilitation Functions

Plyometric training and treatment regimes exist for different functions and methods. From a training standpoint, development from overloads might be

- resistive (forces of gravity, F);
- spatial (range of motion, d); and
- temporal (speed of movement, t).

These overloads exist as a menu of methodologies for improving power [F $\times$ d / t] (Radcliffe and Farentinos 1985).

Treatment regimes also exist for three corresponding methodologies:

- Lengthening, or increasing the resting length of the muscle tendon unit, stretching as a method of developing the tendons
- Loading, or increasing the stress on the tendons by progressive loading for basic physical development
- Contraction speed, or increasing the speed of the movements, thereby increasing the loads on the tendon

Several treatment programs exist that use eccentric exercise. As an example, Curwin and Stanish (1984) suggest this rehabilitation treatment for tendinitis: static stretching, followed by progressive eccentric exercise, determined by the amount of pain or discomfort (they give a symptom classification system), followed once again by static stretching, and concluding with ice massage applied to the inflicted areas.

You may notice that in the progressive development of the stretch-shortening cycle, or in a plyometric training program, some parts of the early drills and exercises, designed to foster correct technical and developmentally safe performance, do not adhere to the definitions of elastic, reactive, or plyometric exercise training. If the goals and objectives of the program are sincere, then we must get beyond this discrepancy so the final outcome—the elite level of progression—is truly explosive, impulsive, elastic-reactive, plyometric, and impressive. As Siff and Verkhoshansky (1996) have pointed out, we need to recognize that we can arrange plyometric training in many categories. Some examples are the distinctions between impact (an eccentric movement that ends in contact with a surface) and nonimpact (no surface contact ending stretch-shortening cycle movements). Distinctions also exist between maximal (producing rebound tensions and impulses of the highest intensities) and submaximal (exhibiting lesser impulses, lower intensities, and being less complex in execution) exercises. These distinctions fit along the stress continuum explained in chapter 4.

Many movements may be preparatory, or supplemental, before progressing to more classical plyometric movements. Again, it is understanding the concepts of the training, the proper lead-up progressions, and evaluating successful execution for advancement that are important to the overall development of the plyometric program.

The primary task in using stretch-shortening cycle and plyometric training is to fully understand the program you want to use it for. You can best accomplish this by establishing goals and objectives. Whatever the program, it's necessary to include certain objectives from the beginning. These objectives are defining the principles of this style of training, balancing and progressing the exercise movements, and applying the principles throughout, so they encompass the entire plan of the program.

Here are examples of these goals and objectives, as they might apply to establishing a program:

1. Develop a well-balanced, well-rounded, progressive training program.
2. Include the stretch-shortening cycle within all applications of basic training development (e.g., preparatory, technical, developmental, and transitional).
3. Use encompassing and individualized planning to safely and successfully progress beginners through to advanced or elite performers.
4. Create a system for evaluating the performance of the program.

Above all, keep in mind that the best training in itself is using proper progressions. If you always check the posture, balance, stability, and flexibility of each athlete throughout, then you produce a great deal more information. This feedback will go far in helping you apply proper dosages and load intensities.

Chapter 4

Lower Body, Legs, and Hips

There is probably no limit to the variety of stretch-shortening cycle exercises that you can devise. Some imagination and inquisitiveness, peppered with a basic understanding of the neuromuscular processes involved, will allow you to develop myriad useful drills. However, it is neither practical nor necessary to identify each movement pattern of every sport skill and design a specific plyometric drill for it. In fact, only a small number of power movements are key in sport. In the next few chapters we present a set of drills for these power movements. Coaches and athletes will see drills that are appropriate for their training needs; our explanations and demonstrations are intended to add a few insights.

The exercises begin with the simple, fundamental drills and progress to the more complex and difficult. As an athlete improves in strength and performance, he or she can advance to the more difficult drills. Coaches, and athletes as well, should determine whether individuals have the skills for properly executing the complex drills using the various apparatuses we mention. Use the proper planning and evaluation criteria for safe and optimal training progression to enhance your sport performance.

In the following chapters, the drills and exercises will proceed in a progression for teaching and learning (see figure 4.1). The methods we employ are exactly the ways in which you should teach and master them, using the sequence, cues, and performance protocols as the guide to moving to the next level of exercises.

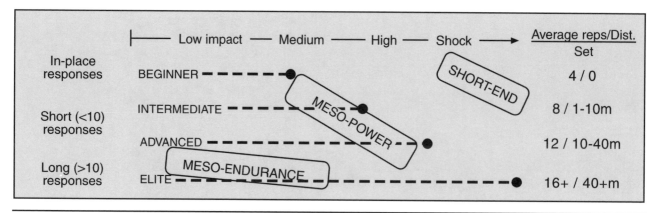

Figure 4.1 The plyometric stress continuum.
1986 Gambetta, Rogers, Seminiek, Fields, and Radcliffe

Training Movements and Methods

We see a variety of movements and action sequences in sports. Some are simple and involve few learned skill components, but others are exceedingly complicated. Within the stretch-shortening cycle, a broad spectrum of simple to complex exercises for training is available. Deciding which exercises to use depends on your athletic performance goals.

As coaches and practitioners, we continually attempt to come closer together in using the proper terminology for types of training. We have introduced several systems for categorizing plyometric exercises based on functional anatomy, their relationship with athletic movements, and competitive events.

In this and the next chapter we separate the exercises based on the musculature involved and how it relates to particular sport movements. We examine the major muscle groups used in movements, the biomechanics basic to many sports, and we provide a rationale for using certain drills, and their respective terminology, to train progressively for more power.

Target Muscle Groups

The exercises here and in chapter 5 are organized along the stress continuum according to three body regions: (1) lower body (legs and hips), (2) trunk (midsection), and (3) upper body (chest, shoulders, shoulder girdle, and arms). Although we consider them separately here, these categories are functionally integrated; they are parts of what we often refer to as the power chain.

Movements and the Power Chain

Most athletic movement originates from the hips and legs. This is true for running, throwing, and jumping actions, which may be the final performance objective or a component of more complex movements. For example, often the energy of motion for the hips and legs transfers up through the midsection by flexing, extending, twisting, or bending. The upper body finally receives the energy to execute some type of skilled movement involving shoulders, chest, and arms.

The organization of plyometric exercises in this chapter follows the power chain concept. Most exercises are specific to leg and hip action because these muscle groups are the center of power for athletic movement and have major involvement in virtually all sports. Here we describe stretch-shortening cycle movements designed to work the musculature of the hips and legs and the specific muscle actions affected.

Jumps

In many programs plyometric training is defined merely as jump training. Many styles and definitions of jumping have been used to describe training and evaluating athletic performance.

In jumping, we seek maximum height, or in teaching terms "projecting the hips upward," but we may not emphasize horizontal distance. Although lead-up footwork can vary, athletes usually perform jumps involving both legs in the takeoff and landing. Track and field literature refers to jumping as any takeoff movement that lands on both feet. This is an excellent description, and, although it does not fit all situations (e.g., high jump), it shows another way of connecting training terms with performance terms. The starting position and initiation methods when jumping for height have significant value. Several types of jumps are distinctive, including the following:

- Squat jump—If the position performed was without a prestretch movement, we can term it a squat jump (SJ), which is executing a vertical jump from a static position of ankle, knee, and hip flexion of specified degrees.

- Countermovement jump—If you perform a prestretch movement, we consider it a countermovement jump (CMJ), which is executing a vertical jump from a preceding flexion of the ankle, knee, and hip joints and subsequently extending the briefly flexed musculoskeletal system.

- Depth (drop) jump—The next term in the progression of jumps in both investigative and developmental exercises is the depth jump, also referred to as drop jump (DJ). It describes the execution of a vertical jump after landing from a drop of a specified height, the flexion or countering of the landing, and the following extension of that musculature.

In explosive power training we can further distinguish applications relating to jumping:

- In-place jumps—The takeoff and landing do not involve horizontal travel. Only a vertical displacement of the body takes place. In-place jumps are usually reserved for beginning exercise progressions, or if advanced, low-intensity and moderate-volume work.

- Long jumps—In track and field terminology some jumping movements may travel horizontally; this definition involves progressions in which takeoffs and landings of low intensity and high volume are recorded in meters rather than contacts. This is a term some coaches use to describe drills that travel great distances (30-100 meters).

- Meso-endurance jumps—This is another track and field coaching education term advocating takeoffs and landings of low intensity and high volume; meso-endurance jumps also are usually qualified in distances (rather than contact repetitions). They describe low-impact, simple bounding, galloping, and combination exercises that travel large distances (40-80 meters).

- Meso-power jumps—Conversely, takeoffs and landings of high intensity and low volume may also be meso-power jumps (another borrowing from track and field terminology), which are exercises using alternating or single-leg contacts, or involving boxes.
- Short-end jumps—We often term takeoffs and landings of low volume and highest (or shock) intensity short-end jumps. These exercises involve a high degree of complexity and high impact, such as hurdle hops, depth jumps, and standing triple jumps. In the context of explosive training, the shock method was originally meant as a description of eccentric training; more specifically though, it referred to the explosive-reactive methods involving impulsive types of training (such as depth jumping).

Bounds

The emphasis in bounding is to gain maximum horizontal distance, with height being a factor in the success of that distance. Athletes perform bounds either with both feet together or in alternate fashion.

In track and field terms, bounding is any movement taking off from one leg and landing on the other. We agree with this term from the standpoint of the advanced execution; however, early progressions of horizontal hip projection encourage the double-leg takeoffs and landings to maintain low stress and emphasize high technical value. Therefore, we will place alterations to the true terminology of bounding in this category (e.g., prancing, galloping, and skipping) for the purposes of teaching and learning progressively.

Hops

The primary emphasis in hopping is to achieve height or distance with a maximum rate of cyclic leg movement. Gaining horizontal distance is of secondary importance in the early training scheme, to emphasize the value of hip projection accompanied with optimal cyclic leg action. Later, de-emphasizing the vertical aspect may become important to accomplish more specific goals (e.g., hop phase of the competitive triple jump).

Again in track and field terms, hopping is described as a takeoff and landing movement from one leg onto the same leg. This term is agreeable with respect to the teaching and performance progression. Especially with the complexity of hops, early progressions require the balance and postural stability of using both legs for good hip projection and cyclic leg action, regardless of the direction (forward, lateral, or backward).

Leaps

Leaping is a single-effort exercise that emphasizes maximum height and horizontal distance. Athletes perform leaps with either one or both legs. Leaping is another description of movements similar to jumping and bounding, usually a single-repetition (nonrepeatable) response.

Skips

Athletes perform skipping by alternating a step-hop of right to right step, then left to left step, emphasizing height and horizontal distance. You can apply this step-hop method in all directions (forward, lateral, and backward).

Ricochet

The emphasis in a ricochet is solely on the rapid rate of leg and foot movement. You minimize vertical and horizontal distance to allow a higher (faster) rate of execution. The plyometric drills, as with many other exercise methodologies, fall under two developmental categories, one is loading or resisted and the other is unloading or assisted. Ricochets, done with the proper feeling of falling, can fit into the latter, or what some term overspeed style of training.

Basic Drills

For basic drills for the legs and hips, we have grouped the exercises into jumps, bounds and skips, and hops. Within each category, we present the exercises in a continuum, from low intensity to moderate, high, and shock. Table 4.1 is a summary of the basic drills for legs and hips. You also find for each drill a description that includes its purpose, starting position, and action sequence.

Table 4.1	Legs and Hips		
Continuum Scaling			
Low	*Moderate*	*High*	*Shock*
Jumps			
Pogo	Double-Leg Butt Kick	Double Scissors Jump	Depth Jump
Squat Jump	Knee-Tuck Jump	Single-Leg Stride Jump	Box Jump (MR)
Box Jump	Split Jump	Stride Jump Crossover	Depth Leap
Rocket Jump	Scissors Jump	Quick Leap	Depth Jump Leap
Star Jump			
Bounds and Skips			
Prancing	Single-Leg Stair Bound	Lateral Bound	
Galloping	Dbl.-Leg Incline & Stair Bound	Alternate Leg Diagonal Bound	
Fast Skipping	Lateral Stair Bound		Box Skip
Ankle Flip	Alternate Leg Stair Bound		Box Bound
Lateral Bound (SR)	Alternate Leg Bound		
Double-Leg Speed Hop			
Hops			
Dbl.-Leg Hop Progression	Angle Hop	Single-Leg Lateral Hop	
Dbl.-Leg Speed Hop	Single-Leg Butt Kick	Decline Hop	
Incremental Vertical Hop	Single-Leg Progression Hop		
Side Hop		Single Leg Speed Hop	
Side Hop-Sprint		Single-Leg Diagonal Hop	
Ricochets			

JUMPS (Drills 1–17)

Drill 1   Pogo

Introduction: This is the beginning exercise in teaching and learning jumps. The posture and the landing and takeoff positions for vertical hip projections begin with these simple lower-leg executions.

Starting position: Take an upright stance with knees slightly bent, chest out, and shoulders back.

Action sequence: Begin by emphasizing a vertical takeoff, projecting the hips upward for height, using only the lower portion of the legs. Use the arms and shoulders in an upward blocking fashion. Emphasize slight flexion and extension of the knee, and more flexion of the ankle and foot. Upon takeoff, the ankle must lock the foot into toes-up position (dorsiflexion), maintaining this locked position throughout to ensure sturdy contacts and quick, elastic takeoffs.

Drill 2   **Squat Jump**

Introduction: This exercise is performed on a flat, semiresilient surface. It is a basic drill for developing power in the legs and hips and applies to many sports. The primary emphasis is to attain maximum height with every effort.

Starting position: Assume a relaxed, upright stance with feet about shoulder-width apart. Interlock the fingers and place the palms against the back of the head. This will assure proper posture for takeoff and landing in the beginning stages of progressive development. Later, as good posture is regularly evident, you can use blocking with the arms and shoulders.

Action sequence: Begin by flexing downward to a half-squat position; immediately check this downward movement and explode upward as high as possible, extending the hips, knees, and ankles to maximum length as quickly as you can. Initially, freeze the landing, check for quality; then you can reset and begin another repetition. Progress from the single response to the multiple with a pause sequence of repetitions, then finally to multiple responses, initiating the jumping phase just before reaching the semisquat position. Work for maximum height with each jump.

Drill 3   **Box Jump** (Single Response)

Introduction: The main use of a box in this capacity is to lessen the forces of impact upon landing, aid in executing good landing mechanics, and provide a target for vertical hip projection.

Starting position: The progression for optimal box jumping relies on an assortment of starting positions approximately an arm's length away from the landing platform. The progression is as follows: (1) Static squat—take a semisquat stance, with feet positioned hip width and arms back in readiness to thrust forward. (2) Countermovement jump—use an upright stance with the same foot positioning, a quick flexion into semisquat, and subsequent explosive take-off. (3) Step—leave one foot in the previous position under the hip, while placing the other foot behind. Bend the knees and shift the weight to the forward foot to avoid any rockerstep action. In pushing off, the back foot creates momentum for the subsequent takeoff upon placement back to its original position. (4) Lateral step bound—positioned approximately one and one-half steps directly to the side of the normal takeoff position, push off with the outside foot and lead with the inside leg into a lateral move to a two-foot takeoff from the original takeoff spot.

Action sequence: Upon takeoff from the progressive starting positions, rapidly extend the hips and knees; quickly and explosively push off the ground, while blocking the arms, into a flexed landing position on the platform.

Drill 4   **Rocket Jump**

Introduction: Perform this exercise on a flat, semiresilient surface. It is a basic drill for developing power throughout the entire torso and applies to many sports. The primary emphasis is to attain maximum height and vertical reach with every effort.

Starting position: Assume a relaxed, upright stance with feet about shoulder-width apart. Slightly flex the arms and hold them close to the body.

Action sequence: Begin by flexing downward to a half-squat position; immediately check this downward movement and explode from this takeoff position upward as high as possible, extending the whole body vertically. As the body descends, flex the joints so the body is again poised in takeoff position upon landing. Repeat this flexion to full height extension with minimal movement away from the vertical plane.

Drill 5   **Star Jump**

Introduction: This is a basic drill for developing power throughout the torso and applies to many sports. The primary emphasis is to attain maximum height and attain reach and outward extension with every effort. This is a good beginning drill for work on coordinated movements involving hang time.

Starting position: Assume a relaxed, upright stance with feet about shoulder-width apart. Slightly flex the arms and hold them close to the body.

Action sequence: Begin this movement exactly as the previous exercise; immediately check this downward movement and explode from this takeoff position upward as high as possible, extending the whole body vertically. The difference is that you extend the limbs outward in all four directions away from the body. As the body descends, flex the joints back inward, positioning the body again in takeoff position upon landing.

Drill 6   **Double-Leg Butt Kick**

Introduction: Athletes use this drill as the first of many movements that practice the transfer of force. In other words, you apply more forces by following extension with flexion during flight, using the simple act of flexing the knee joint to allow upward lift with the lower leg.

Starting position: Take an upright stance with knees slightly bent, chest out, and shoulders back.

Action sequence: Using a quick countermovement jump, extend the hips for vertical height and, upon full extension, tuck the toes up and pull the heels upward and slightly backward into the buttocks. The knees will have a minimal rise upward and forward but not in a tuck manner. Maintain posture and upright position by blocking with the arms.

Drill 7   **Knee-Tuck Jump**

Introduction: Do the knee-tuck jump on a resilient, flat surface such as grass or a gymnastic floor mat. Perform this drill in the usual progression of single response (SR), multiple response (MR) with pause, and finally the main MR method.

Starting position: Assume a comfortable upright stance, placing the hands palms down at chest height. Do this in the early stages to assure good takeoff and landing posture and to give the knees a target. Once good posture is regular, use the customary blocking method.

Action sequence: Begin by rapidly dipping down to about the quarter-squat level and immediately explode upward. Drive the knees high toward the chest and attempt to touch them to the palms of the hands. Upon landing, repeat the sequence, each time driving the knees upward and tucking the feet under the body. Perform multiple responses at a rapid rate with minimal ground contact.

Drill 8   **Split Jump**

Introduction: Perform split jumps on a flat surface. They are especially good for developing striding power for running and cross-country skiing; they are also specific to the split portion of the jerk.

Starting position: Assume a stance with one leg extended forward with the knee over the midpoint of the foot and the other leg back with the knee bent and underneath the plumb line of the hips and shoulders.

Action sequence: Jump as high and straight up as possible. Block with the arms to gain additional lift. Upon landing, retain the spread-legged position, bending the knees to absorb the shock. It is important to keep the shoulders back and in line with the hips to maintain proper stability. Continue the motion for the required repetitions, then switch legs and perform them again with the opposite leg forward.

Drill 9

Scissors Jump

Introduction: As in the split jump, this exercise works the muscles of the lower body and torso. It is similar to the split jump except that you also emphasize leg speed; therefore, it is especially good for runners and jumpers.

Starting position: The beginning stance of the scissors jump is the same as that of the split jump.

Action sequence: The initial movement of the scissors jump is identical to that of the split jump. However, at the apex of the jump, reverse the position of the legs, that is, front to back and back to front. Switching the legs occurs in midair, and you must do it quickly before landing. Upon landing in MR mode, repeat the jump, again reversing the position of the legs. Emphasize attaining maximal vertical height and leg speed in this exercise.

Drill 10   **Double Scissors Jump**

Introduction: A variation of the scissors jump for the more advanced athlete is the **double scissors jump** (not shown). This drill is excellent for working the flexion and extension muscles that involve the hips, legs, and torso.

Starting position: The position is the same as for split and scissors jumps.

Action sequence: In the double scissors jump, once you reach the apex of the jump, attempt a complete cycle of the legs, front to back, back to front, and vice versa while in the air, landing with the legs in their original position. The jumper must remember to keep excellent shoulders-above-hips posture. Perform this double-switch movement about the hips, involving total-leg movements and not merely switching lower legs or feet. Therefore, perform this exercise in the single-response mode only.

Drill 11   Single-Leg Stride Jump

Introduction: You will need a long, sturdy bench, rectangular box, or a row of bleachers or stadium steps for the single-leg stride jump. This drill is excellent for any sport or activity that requires good projection of the hips from a singular or alternating leg movement. The idea behind this drill is to place the hips and one leg so you increase the stride without changing proper posture and technique. In terms of projection, this would be similar to working up a hill.

Starting position: Assume a position to the side and at one end of the bench. Place the inside foot on top of the bench, and hold arms downward at the sides.

Action sequence: Begin the exercise with an upward movement of the arms; then using an initial push from both legs, followed by using the inside leg (foot on bench) for power, jump upward as high as possible. In MR mode, move slightly forward down the bench, repeat the action as soon as the outside leg (away from the bench) touches the ground. Use mainly the inside leg for power and support, allowing the outside leg to contact the ground with minimal time and maximal impulse. Once you reach the end of the bench, turn around, and reversing the leg positions, repeat the sequence in the other direction. Remember to gain full height and body extension with each jump.

Drill 12   **Stride Jump Crossover**

Introduction: For this drill, you will need the same type of equipment we described in the single-leg stride jump. This drill advances the multiple-response effects of the single-leg stride jump more specifically for running, jumping, gymnastics, and similar sport events with the alternating aspects.

Starting position: As in the single-leg stride jump, assume a standing position at one end of the bench with one foot on the ground and the other on the bench. Arms should be down at the sides.

Action sequence: Initiate the movement by rapidly blocking the arms upward. Continue this upward momentum by driving off the bench with the elevated leg, jumping as high as possible, and extending the body fully. At this point, carry the body over the bench and slightly forward so the driving leg touches the ground on the opposite side of the bench and the trailing leg rests on top of the bench. Orientation of the body and position of the feet are now opposite that of the original starting position. As soon as the original driving leg contacts the ground, repeat the motion but with the original trailing leg acting as the major power source. Repeat these movements back and forth the length of the bench. Work to achieve maximum height with each jump, using the arms to assist in lifting the body. Minimize ground- and bench-contact time with the feet; perform the movements as quickly as possible.

Drill 13 **Quick Leap**

Introduction: You will need a soft landing surface, such as grass, sand, or a wrestling mat, and a bench, stool, or box approximately 12 to 24 inches high for the quick leap drill. This exercise is useful in volleyball, football, basketball, platform diving, and weightlifting.

Starting position: With feet together, assume a semierect position facing the box (about an arm's length away). Keep the arms at the sides and slightly bent at the elbows.

Action sequence: Leap toward the box by exploding powerfully out of the starting position with the help of an energetic arm swing. While moving through the air, prepare for takeoff by

assuming a semisquat position, keeping the knees high and forward of the hips, and tucking the feet under the hips. Upon landing, full footed and with locked ankle on the box, immediately thrust forward again, this time extending and straightening the entire body. Finish by landing full footed on the ground, bending your legs to act as a cushion. Make the initial jump to the box as quickly as possible with just enough height to reach the box. Anticipate and concentrate on the second explosion from the box; stress a full extension of the body after takeoff. You can perform a variation of this exercise by landing on the box with only one foot, thus executing the leap with one driving leg.

Drill 14 | **Depth Jump**

Introduction: You will need an elevated surface (box or bench) approximately 12 to 36 inches high for this exercise. The landing surface should be forgiving, yet resilient; grass, gymnastic flooring, or cushioned turf work well. The depth jump is a shock-method exercise and comes in the final portion of the training continuum. Therefore, progression into this drill is a must, as well as progression within it. Apply the shock method by using the elevated platform and a drop or fall to the takeoff surface. The key is to not initiate a rhythm of landing. The landing is the precise phase we are negotiating, to create as efficient a performance as possible. This requires handling the surprise of landing and subsequent takeoff in as optimal an execution as possible. This aspect makes the depth jump elite in its application to all sports because it employs leg strength, speed, and quickness. It also can be a source of problems if you do not progress into it properly, as described in chapter 3.

Starting position: Begin by standing at the edge of the elevated platform with the front of the feet just over the edge. Keep the knees slightly bent and arms relaxed at the sides. The objective of this position is to slide or fall off the edge, rather than to jump or step off and inadvertently set the rhythm of performance.

Action sequence: Drop from the elevated surface to the ground. As the flight of the drop occurs, prepare for landing by flexing at the knees and hips. Cock the elbows back and dorsiflex the ankles. Progression into the drill begins with repetitions of landing only. As you arrive at a proper landing position, you can progress to the efficient efforts of immediate takeoff. In depth jumping, it is upon landing, not after, that you initiate the jumping phase by thrusting the arms upward and extending the body for as much height as possible. You need maximum intensity and effort to gain optimal benefits in producing force while keeping ground-contact time to a minimum. Plenty of rest between each maximum effort is necessary as well.

Drill 15   **Box Jump** (Multiple Response)

Introduction: For this exercise you will need boxes, benches, or a sturdy, elevated platform between 12 and 24 inches high.

Starting position: Assume a relaxed stance facing the box or platform approximately an arm's length away. Arms should be down at the sides and legs slightly bent.

Action sequence: Using the arms to aid in the initial burst, jump upward and forward, landing with feet simultaneously on top of the box or platform. Immediately drop or jump back down to the original starting place; then repeat the sequence. You can perform a variation of these responsive movements by alternating the directions of jumping and dropping onto and off the platform. Remember to block with the arms and shoulders and concentrate on minimizing contact times without the expense of good hip projection.

Drill 16   **Depth Leap**

Introduction: This progression is to provide more of an elastic and reactive execution than the normal countermove leap.

Starting position: Begin in the same position as the depth jump.

Action sequence: Drop or fall from the elevated surface, landing in take-off position, and initiate takeoff immediately upon touchdown. The leap is performed by gaining distance and height outward. The leap is a single, intense effort; therefore it is helpful to have a pit of sand or foam to cushion the landings.

Drill 17   **Depth Jump Leap**

Introduction: For this drill you need two boxes or benches, one 12 to 16 inches high and the other 22 to 26 inches high. Use a resilient landing surface such as grass or a thin mat. This drill applies to weightlifting, basketball, volleyball, ski jumping, and platform diving.

Starting position: Stand on one of the two boxes with arms at the sides; feet should be together and slightly off the edge as in the depth jump. Place the other box approximately two or three feet in front of and facing the performer.

Action sequence: Begin by dropping off the initial box as in depth jumping, landing and simultaneously taking off with both feet. Jump onto the higher box, landing on both feet (or on one foot if you are advanced), and drive upward and forward as intensely as possible, using the arms and a full extension of the body. Complete the motion by landing on both feet with legs flexed to cushion the impact. Concentrate on a quick, explosive depth jump, overcoming the force of landing and using the recoil to leap to the higher box. Think of driving hard off the higher box with the landing leg. As with other shock exercises, you will need maximum rest periods of one to two minutes or more.

BOUNDS AND SKIPS (Drills 18-31)

Drill 18   Prancing

Introduction: As pogo is for jumps, prancing is the beginning progression for bounding. Project the hips horizontally off a two-foot landing and takeoff. It is important to perform this drill with takeoffs and landings on both feet simultaneously.

Starting position: Assume a standing position with a slight knee bend and the hips tilted forward.

Action sequence: Upon takeoff, push the hips outward and upward with the knee of one leg recovering forward. Upon landing, repeat the takeoff with the opposite knee recovering forward. The upper body action is the same as in running. For both feet to land simultaneously, the ankles must remain locked in a toes-up position.

Drill 19   **Galloping**

Introduction: Galloping is a rhythmic exercise that fosters good hip projection and back leg push-off. Lead leg mechanics and proper pawing or leg cycle mechanics are a secondary emphasis.

Starting position: Assume a standing position with one leg in front of the other.

Action sequence: Begin by pushing off with the back leg and foot, keeping the ankle locked to emphasize a spring-loaded

landing and takeoff. Continue to keep the same leg behind the hips and project the hips forward, while maintaining the opposite leg in a forward position for initial landing and balance within each stride. After executing 6 to 12 repetitions, switch the position of the legs and repeat the sequence. Emphasize hip projection upward and forward with forceful, quick extensions of the back knee and ankle, accompanied by light, cyclic striding actions of the lead leg.

Drill 20 **Fast Skipping**

Introduction: Skipping is an excellent drill for working the striding muscles. The progressions reinforce sprinting and jumping mechanics and train the explosiveness athletes need in the acquisition stages. Perform all skipping by executing a step-hop pattern of right-right-step to left-left-step to right-right-step, and so on.

Starting position: Assume a relaxed standing position with one leg slightly forward.

Action sequences: Perform fast skipping by maintaining close contact with the ground and eliminating air time. Perform this sequence at as fast a rhythm as possible, driving the lead leg toes up, the knee forward and upward, and keeping the heel up under the hips. Do not emphasize stride distances; maximum thigh extension, recovery, and frequency are premium.

Drill 20a   **Extended Skipping**

Perform extended skipping by allowing a long flight time with each hop and step of the sequence. The step phase must maintain good stride mechanics while the hop foot covers as much distance as possible to accompany the maximum horizontal knee drive and lead-foot pawing action. Extended skipping is similar to the timing and rhythm of the triple jump.

Perform **power skipping** (not shown) by driving off the back leg, initiating a short, skipping step; then, with the opposite leg, thrust the toe and knee up. Upon landing repeat the action with the opposite leg. Obtain as much height and explosive power as possible after each short step. Drive the knee up hard and fast to transfer force from maximal extension off the support leg. Block with the arms, concentrating on lift and hang time of the body while minimizing the ground-contact time.

Drill 21 **Ankle Flip**

Introduction: Because you perform the ankle flip from one leg onto the other leg, it is the next level in the progression toward bounding. The ankle flip emphasizes forward hip projection through full extension of the hip and knee.

Starting position: Assume a relaxed, upright stance with one foot forward.

Action sequence: Begin by pushing the hips forward and outward from the lead foot and leg. With minimal knee flexion and the ankle locked, land with the opposite foot, and quickly extend from that position so the hips remain in a forward thrusting sequence with the ankle always projecting from slightly behind.

Drill 22 **Lateral Bound**
(Single Response)

Introduction: Do the beginning progression of the lateral bound as a single-response drill, using maximum explosion and resetting each time for optimal feedback about your performance. Emphasize using the thigh and groin muscles as well as the hips and lower back.

Starting position: Assume a semisquat position that is perpendicular to the destination.

Action sequence: Emphasizing distance and horizontal trajectory, allow the lead leg to do a countermovement jump inward, shifting the weight to the outside leg for an immediate push-off and extension while the lead shoulder and knee dip and drive for distance. The lead foot will land first with the trail foot following to balance the landing.

Drill 23   **Single-Leg Stair Bound**

Introduction: The single-leg stair bound uses the decreased impact of landing on an elevated surface while attending to the mechanics needed for optimal execution. A set of closed stairs, those having facing panels (stadium steps, etc., not bleachers), are necessary to ensure that the lead foot avoids catching underneath.

Starting position: Balance on one leg on the second step up, with the opposite leg poised slightly behind you and above the step adjacently below.

Action sequence: Come off the top leg, drop down to the step below and onto the opposite leg. When the back foot contacts the lower step, immediately explode and push off, simultaneously driving the original lead knee upward and onto a step or two above the original starting step. This right leg, drop to left, bound up onto right, galloping sequence continues for allotted repetitions. Then repeat by switching the lead and push-off legs (left, drop to right, bound to left, etc.) to complete a whole set.

Drill 24   **Double-Leg Incline and Stair Bound**

Introduction: Perform this drill on closed stairs, stadium steps, or a sloped hill. By working up the incline we reduce the impact of landing forces and place greater emphasis on extension and takeoff forces.

Starting position: Assume a relaxed, semisquat stance on the front portion of the step. Relax the arms and hold them slightly behind the body in preparation for blocking.

Action sequence: A progression exists, as for many other exercises. Perform the single-response mode on stairs or a hill. Do a countermovement jump into full extension and explosion forward and upward *into* the incline, followed by flexion into proper, full-foot postural landings, resetting between each repetition. It is best to perform multiple-response bounds on steps. From the ready position, drop back onto the previous step to initiate movement. The drop should maintain a posture that allows hip projection upward and forward. With as rapid a takeoff as possible, bound up as many steps as good landing technique will allow, ready to drop and take off again.

Drill 25   **Lateral Stair Bound**

Introduction:

This is the progressive combination of a multiple-response version of the lateral bound on the decreased landing impact of elevated surfaces. Like the single-leg stair bound, this exercise uses the dropping back of one step and explosive sideways bounding action up several more.

Starting position:

Begin in a semisquat stance with shoulders perpendicular to the stairs and the weight on the upstairs leg.

Action sequence:

In the same manner as the other stair bound exercises, keep the weight shifted *into* the steps, drop back one step with the downside leg, and, with immediate extension of that leg and knee, drive off the upside leg, quickly bound upward and inward two or three steps. Continue this drop one, bound two or three up for 8 to 12 repetitions; then repeat facing the opposite direction.

Drill 26   Alternate Leg Stair Bound

Introduction: Next in the progression of horizontal hip projection is alternate leg landing of decreased impact using incline surfaces such as hills or enclosed stairs.

Starting position: Assume a stance similar to that of beginning to sprint.

Action sequence: Begin by running up the steps, with maximum extension of the support leg and maximum knee drive of the swing leg, forward and *into* the stairs. Maintain toes-up, heels-up posture for quick takeoffs and explosiveness, while refraining from overstriding and lengthy time on each step.

Drill 27 — **Alternate Leg Bound**

Introduction: This drill is the prime exercise in specifically developing explosive leg and hip power. Alternating the legs works the flexor and extensor muscles of the thighs and hips, a drill that enhances running, sprinting, and jumping actions.

Starting position: Assume a comfortable stance with one foot slightly ahead of the other as to initiate a step; arms should be relaxed and at the sides. Variations to a stationary start are walking or running starts, which assist the efficiency of the performance. Other variations include alternating the landings (e.g., RRL, LLR, RRLL) to emphasize the acceleration-reacceleration of the stride mechanics.

Action sequence: Begin by pushing off with the back leg, driving the knee forward and upward to gain as much height and distance as possible before landing. Repeat the sequence (driving with the other leg) upon landing. Keep the ankle locked in dorsiflexion and the heel up under the hips to reduce the ground-contact time and promote efficient hip projection upon subsequent takeoff. Either block with the arms in a contralateral motion, as with normal running, or execute a double-arm swing.

Drill 28 **Lateral Bound**
(Multiple Response)

Introduction: You can do this drill on flat ground or with angled boxes or a similar incline. This exercise emphasizes using the adductors and abductors of the thighs as well as stabilizing muscles of knees and ankles. The lateral bound is excellent for most sports, especially skating, hockey, Nordic skiing, tennis, basketball, and baseball.

Starting position: Begin in the same position as for the single-response version of this drill. If using an angled box or incline, place it approximately one long step away and at the side.

Action sequence: Push off with the outside foot moving laterally and concentrate on obtaining distance. Upon landing, drive off again in the opposite direction, quickly and powerfully, returning to the distance you began. Continue this back and forth maneuver for similar repetitions.

Drill 29 **Alternate Leg Diagonal Bound**

Introduction: A variation of the normal bounding pattern with specific aid in power cutting maneuvers (lateral change of direction by planting the outside foot) offers the ability to gain distance at angles as well as forward.

Starting position: Begin in the same position as normal bounding.

Action sequence: Perform this drill in the same manner as the alternate leg bound, but increase the distance from side to side as well as forward upon landings.

Drill 30　**Box Skip**

Introduction: You need two to four boxes in heights of 8 to 24 inches for this exercise. This is an advanced shock-method drill for elite practitioners involved in jumping events such as track and field, basketball, and volleyball.

Starting position: Place the boxes in any order of height about 6 to 10 feet apart. Facing the first box from about two steps away, assume an upright stance with one leg slightly behind the other. Arms should be relaxed at the sides.

Action sequence: Drive off the back leg, attempting to gain as much height with the hips as possible. Block with the arms and drive the knee upward to assist in the explosive extension of the push-off leg. Immediately upon landing on the box, drive the other leg forward and upward, gaining maximum height and distance. Use momentum from this action to leap from the first box. Make the ground landing between the first and second boxes with the same leg as the landing on the first box; then step to the next box, thus the skip. This skip action sequence continues over the remaining boxes. Concentrate on push-off and knee drive with quickness and maximum force, for liftoff and hang time.

Drill 31 **Box Bound**

Introduction: By using boxes as with the previous drill, we can place more resistive overloads on the specific sprinting and jumping musculature. Because this exercise is of shock mode, use it at the advanced stages of training with highly competent athletes of high-training maturity. This explains why it is last in this segment's continuum of exercises.

Starting position: Assume the same stance as the alternate leg bound, two to three steps in front of a series of boxes spaced according to the participant's abilities as well as technique considerations.

Action sequence: The execution is the same as for the alternate leg bound except that you make every other step from a box. Emphasize landing and foot placement that maintain an erect torso and allow immediate forward hip projection. Eliminate landing positions that foster overstriding or pulling the hips over and off the box.

Hops (Drills 32-43)

Drill 32   Double-Leg Hop Progression

Introduction:

To properly execute the hop exercises, use a teaching and performance progression. Develop proper takeoff and landing mechanisms, and remain consistent throughout. Using cones or small hurdles helps foster the technique in the beginning stages.

Starting position:

Assume a relaxed, standing position with knees slightly bent and arms at sides. Stand directly in front of a series of three to five hurdles spaced approximately three feet apart.

Action sequence:

Using a quick countermovement jump, extend the hips for vertical height, and upon full extension, tuck the toes, knees, and heels upward in a cycling motion to clear the hurdle. Maintain posture and upright position by blocking with the arms. The execution progression is as follows: Single-response hop—upon clearing the first

hurdle, land with full-foot contact and give at the knees and hips. After sticking this landing, pause, then reset the body position, stance, and relationship to the next hurdle. Then execute the next hop. This reset allows for a re-education of landing and takeoff technique.

Multiple-response hops with pause—in all forms of athletic movement, how well you land dictates how well you take off. Execute these hops by pausing for a brief moment, in as proper a landing position as possible, then performing the next takeoff without having to reset the lower or upper body to be successful. Once the takeoffs from pause are successful, then progress to multiple responses (see Drill 33, the double-leg speed hop).

Drill 33 **Double-Leg Speed Hop**

Introduction: This exercise builds speed and power in the muscles of the legs and hips. It is a useful exercise for developing explosiveness and specifically applies to the mechanics of speed work required in running.

Starting position: Begin in the same position as the double-leg hop progression.

Action sequence: Begin the action exactly as in the double-leg hop progression. Upon each landing, take off quickly upward again with the same cycling action of the legs. Execute the action sequence as rapidly as possible. Work for height and distance, but not at the expense of repetition rate.

Drill 34 **Incremental Vertical Hop**

Introduction: For this exercise you will need a rope or elastic tubing approximately 15 feet long. Attach one end to a wall or pole at eye level and the other end to a semireleasable object at ground level. This drill is excellent for all activities as it aids in stability during explosive cycling action.

Starting position: Assume a relaxed position immediately to the side of the lowest end of the tubing with feet together, facing the wall or pole. Prepare the arms for blocking to provide lift.

Action sequence: Hopping back and forth over the tubing, advance up the tubing as high as possible. Bring the knees forward and upward toward the chest while tucking the feet underneath the hips. Continue up the tubing as far as possible, thus completing the set.

Drill 35 **Side Hop**

Introduction: This exercise uses two cones approximately 18 to 26 inches high. The movement specifically enhances explosive lateral power throughout the legs and hips. This drill is useful for all activities employing lateral movement.

Starting position: Set both cones side by side approximately two feet apart; you can progressively expand the distance with increased performance. Assume a relaxed, upright stance to the outside of one cone. Keep the feet together, pointing straight ahead, and cock the arms ready to provide lift and aid in balance.

Action sequence: From the starting position, take off sideways over the first cone, then the second one. Without hesitating, change direction by jumping back over the second cone, then the first one; continue this back-and-forth sequence. Block with the arms in an upward thrusting motion to aid in lift and posture.

Drill 36   **Side Hop-Sprint**

Introduction: You need a low bench, bag, tackling dummy, or similar object to hop over for this drill. This is a combination exercise going from a series of hops to a full sprint for a short, accelerated distance. It practices the coordination you need for a rapid change of direction. This drill applies to tennis, basketball, baseball, football, and many other sports using change of direction.

Starting position: Stand on one side of the bag with feet together and pointing straight ahead. (A second position that you can progress into is having your back to the bag, toes pointing directly away from it.)

Action sequence: Begin by hopping sideways back and forth over the bag for a designated number of repetitions (approximately six). Execute the hops as rapidly and efficiently as possible. This is a primary objective of the drill, as the emphasis is not the height of the hops but rather the rate of execution. Keep the trunk and hips centered over the bag, as posture is of prime importance to optimal execution. Anticipate the landing on the last repetition; land in a sprint start posture and accelerate forward past a designated finish line. Several participants using several bags can race, with the participant completing the designated number of hops first having an advantage in finishing first.

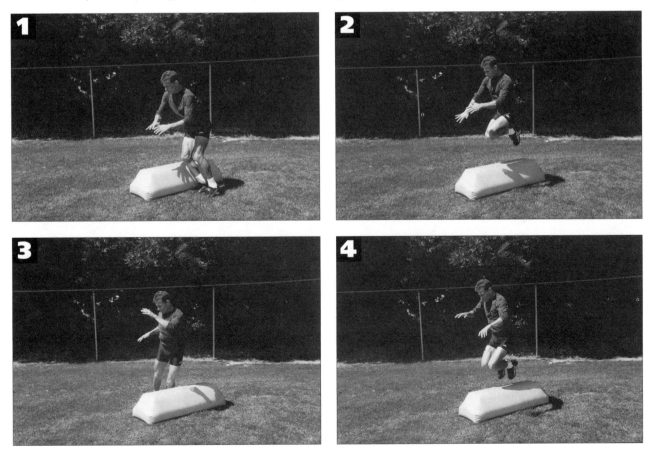

Drill 37 — **Angle Hop**

Introduction: Do this drill preferably on a multiple-angle box or similar apparatus, which you must securely attach to the ground so it does not move or slip while you are performing the hops. The angle hops improve balance and lateral movement. This drill is useful in Alpine skiing, tennis, football, and gymnastics, as well as other sports.

Starting position: Stand in a relaxed position on one angled surface of the box.

Action sequence: Hop laterally from one side of the box to the next sequentially, emphasizing a rapid side-to-side motion. Once skill has improved, progress to more distant angles. Block with the arms for balance.

Drill 38 **Single-Leg Butt Kick**

Introduction: This drill is the first of many movements that practice using one leg in explosive actions. It has prime value to all sprinting and single-leg jumping activities. This drill is also excellent for determining an athlete's ability to handle the posture, balance, stability, and flexibility of single-leg work.

Starting position: Take an upright stance with knees slightly bent, chest out, and shoulders back. Lift one leg by pulling the heel upward and only slightly backward to the buttocks.

Action sequence: Using a quick countermovement jump, extend the hips for vertical height, and upon full extension, tuck the toes and heel of the takeoff leg upward and slightly backward into the buttocks. The knee will have a minimal rise upward and forward but not in a tuck manner. Maintain posture and upright position by blocking with the arms. In the same single-response, to multiple-response with pause, to multiple-response progression, perform all the repetitions with one leg, then switch to the other.

Drill 39 **Single-Leg Hop Progression**

Introduction: The same progression that applied for the double-leg hop progression applies to advancing to hopping in its most common terminology, with a single leg. The need for optimal posture, balance, stability, and flexibility evaluation is even more present with one-leg landings and takeoffs.

Starting position: Assume a relaxed standing position with knees slightly bent and arms at sides. Completely balance on one leg while maintaining the off leg in a flexed position with the toes up, knee up in front of the body, and the heel up underneath the hip.

Action sequence: Using the countermoving effects of the swing leg for lift and drive, execute the hops in the same manner as the double-leg hop progression.

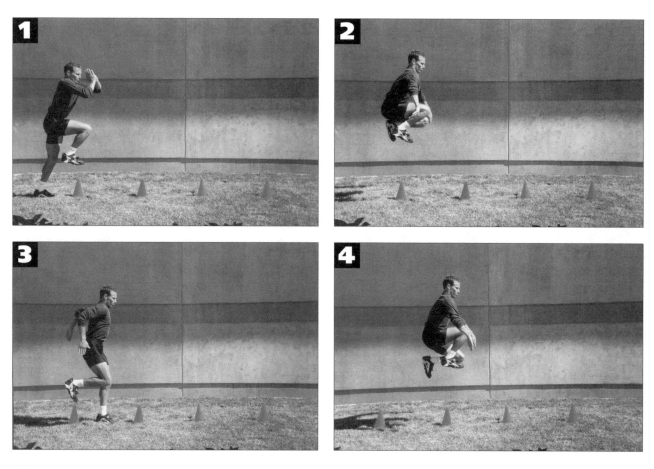

Drill 40 Single-Leg Speed Hop

Introduction: The multiple-response version of true hopping is the ultimate drill for developing the explosive, reactive, and cyclic action of sprinting. The requirements are the same as for the single-leg hop progression.

Starting position: Begin in the same position as the single-leg hop progression.

Action sequence: Use the multiple-response action of rapid yet fully explosive cyclic action for height and distance. Display the locked ankle, heel up, and fast recovering action necessary for optimal execution.

Drill 41 **Single-Leg Diagonal Hop**

Introduction: This drill is slightly higher in stress load than the single-leg hop progression due to the lateral stability necessary to perform these takeoffs and landings.

Starting position: Begin in the same position as the single-leg hop progression.

Action sequence: Upon takeoff, project the hips at a 45-degree angle inside or outside the takeoff point. Progress from sets of three to five repetitions in the outer direction, to sets in the inside direction, then finally to crossing back and forth.

Drill 42 **Single-Leg Lateral Hop**

Introduction: This is an excellent drill for lateral movement and improving the execution of speed and power cutting in athletic movements.

Starting position: Assume the same stance as the single-leg hop progression.

Action sequence: Upon takeoff, project the hips directly to the side of the takeoff point. Then execute the vertical lift and cyclic action in repetitions of three to five, to the outside, inside, or back and forth.

Drill 43 **Decline Hop**

Introduction: Use a grassy hill of about one- to three-degrees inclination. (Note: Do not attempt this exercise on steps, bleachers, or a wet, slick surface.) This drill is an overspeed method of developing elastic reactivity in the lower body through increased shock on the musculature and the increased speed of the downward momentum.

Starting position: Assume a quarter-squat stance at the top of the hill with the body facing down the fall line.

Action sequence: Execute this movement the same as all other forward hopping movements. However, performing this hop on the decline requires even greater emphasis on repetition rate and speed of movement. The single-leg decline hop (photos 1b-3b) is suggested only *after* you master all other hop methods.

Drill 44 **Incline Ricochet**

Introduction: For the ricochets, a set of stairs or stadium steps is required. The stairs must be solid, with no openings for toes and feet to become entrapped. This exercise is designed for practicing reflexive quickness in more of an unloaded or "overspeed" manner. It is well suited for all sports involving fast footwork.

Starting position: Face the bottom of the steps in a relaxed upright position with feet together and arms to the sides and cocked at the elbows.

Action sequence: Rapidly move up every step at the highest rate possible without tripping. Use the arms for balance, keeping thumbs up, and also for assisting in explosion from step to step. Quickness is most important in this drill, so relaxation should be stressed. Anticipate hopping or stepping rapidly to each succeeding step. Think of being light on the feet. Variations of the ricochet can be accomplished by angling to the right or left of the steps or facing completely sideways. The ricochet can be done with feet together (photos 1-2), in carioka step fashion (photos 3-5), with a four-step sequence, or single leg for the advanced.

Chapter 5

Trunk and Upper Body

Continuing along the power chain, we move to the trunk, or torso, shoulder girdle and shoulders, and the arms. For our purposes, the structural definition of the trunk is the midsection of the body, specifically the abdominal and lumbar regions. The torso is the trunk of the body including the chest, shoulders, and pelvic region. The drills for the trunk improve power throughout the torso by developing the flexion, extension, and rotation techniques and the posture, balance, stability, and flexibility that apply to all sport activities.

Training Movements and Methods

Trunk movements include these main categories:
- Swings are movements of the trunk that are lateral, horizontal, or vertical, with secondary involvement of the shoulders, chest, and arms.
- Twists are movements of the torso that are torque or are lateral (or both); they do not involve the shoulders and arms in a major way, but rotate the pelvis and spine.
- Tosses and passes are projecting movements of the upper torso and limbs that take place below or in front of the head (or both). In tossing, the functional

anatomy is identical to the movements of swinging, twisting, and combinations of these.

- Throws are projecting movements of the upper torso and limbs that occur above, over, or across (or both over and across) the head.

Target Muscle Groups

In many sports, we can see the result of the power the hips and legs generate and transfer through the midsection as actions involving the chest, shoulders, back, and arms. So throwing, catching, pushing, pulling, and swinging movements are primarily upper-body activities. With careful analysis, however, we see that these movements demonstrate how important the trunk, hips, and legs are for initial power production, support, weight transfer, and balance.

Thrusts, throws, strokes, passes, and swings all engage various muscle groups of the upper body. The relative degree of arm movement differentiates these action sequences. In their functional anatomy, these movements are similar and involve integrated flexion, extension, and abduction of the arms, as well as support of the arms and shoulder girdle throughout flexion and extension.

Trunk (Drills 45–58)

We will first present 15 drills for the trunk (see table 5.1), then move to 9 drills (and several variations) for the upper body (see table 5.2, p. 115).

Table 5.1   **Trunk Drills**

Continuum Scaling			
Low	*Moderate*	*High*	*Shock*
MB over and under	Bar twist	Vertical swing	
MB half twist	Twist toss	Leg toss	
MB full twist	MB scoop throw	MB scoop toss (MR)	
Shovel toss	Floor kip	Multiple hops to overhead throw	
MB scoop toss (SR)	Horizontal swing	Multiple hops to underhand toss	
MB = medicine ball			

Drill 45   **Medicine Ball Over and Under**

Introduction: The purpose of this drill is to establish a postural sequence of balance and stability in flexion and extension as a preparation for further tossing and throwing exercises.

Starting position: Using a 5- to 15-pound ball, stand with feet approximately shoulder-width apart and your back to the partner or wall. The feet are flat and knees maintain a slight bend. Hold your arms long, chest out, and hips back.

Action sequence: Pass the ball back and forth over the head and between the legs while maintaining a chest-out posture and full-foot contact stability. After performing sets of 10 to 15 repetitions, switch from receiving over (or under) to passing.

Drill 46a   **Medicine Ball Half Twist**

Introduction: This is a beginning postural sequence with progressive balance and stability techniques for rotation.

Starting position: Begin in the same position as the medicine ball over and under, with feet flat and approximately shoulder-width, knees bent, and chest out. Stand back to back with a partner or wall.

Action sequence: Hold the ball in front of the trunk and pass it to the partner or to meet a wall located to each side. Open the hips and turn the shoulders to give and accept the ball. Keep the feet in full contact with the ground while emphasizing posture and flexibility throughout the rotation. One partner turns and passes the ball to a side while the other turns to the same side to receive it.

Drill 46b **Medicine Ball Full Twist**

Introduction: The next sequence increases complexity in the postural progression that involves rotational flexibility.

Starting position: The starting position is the same as for the medicine ball half twist.

Action sequence: The posture, stability, and balance remain similar to the medicine ball half twist. The difference is in the flexibility with the increased degree of rotation. With the medicine ball full twist, both partners turn in the same direction, one to pass, the other to receive.

Drill 47   **Shovel Toss (Single Response)**

Introduction: This drill is a torso extension exercise emphasizing the hip and shoulder joints. Excellent for any athlete who has to explode out of blocks or a stance.

Starting position: Again using a 5- to 15-pound ball, begin on both knees and place the ball on the ground directly in front. Keep your chest out, hips high and back, and position the shoulders in front of the ball.

Action sequence: With arms long and relaxed, the athlete tosses the ball like a line drive as far and fast as possible by quickly thrusting the hips and extending the trunk, executing a scooping or shoveling action, then catching himself in push-up position. Emphasize a full extension of the hip and shoulder action, not arm action.

Drill 48a Medicine Ball Scoop Toss (Single Response)

Introduction: This extension exercise involves lower-body stability and extreme follow-through in extension to the point of body elevation off the ground. This is an excellent accompanying exercise to any Olympic-style pulling movement (e.g., snatch and clean).

Starting position: Assume a semisquat stance. Place the ball on the ground and between the legs, grasping it on either side with fingers spread. Extend your arms, keep your head up and back straight.

Action sequence: Begin by thrusting the hips forward and moving the shoulders upward while maintaining full extension of the arms. Scoop the ball upward, attempting to elevate both the body and the ball to maximum heights. Allow the ball to drop, and begin again.

Drill 48b **Medicine Ball Scoop Toss Variation**

Action sequence: The next progression begins with holding the ball at arm's length just below the waist and executing the toss from a quick, countermovement jump action. The ball remains directly below the shoulders and at arm's length. Execute the countermovement jump by flexing at the hips and knees to produce a more forceful extension and toss release.

Drill 49   **Bar Twist**

Introduction: Use a weighted bar of 20 to 50 pounds in this drill. Concentrate the movement on the trunk musculature, with slight involvement of the shoulders and little of the arms. This is an initial rotational exercise involving the ability to counter a loaded movement direction quickly and forcefully. It is extremely applicable to the throwing and swinging activities of football, baseball, softball, golf, and track and field.

Starting position: Standing upright, place the bar on the shoulders and hold it securely with both hands as far from the center as possible. Bend the knees and place the feet slightly more than shoulder-width apart.

Action sequence: Twist the upper body in one direction; then before the torso is fully rotated, initiate the action in the opposite direction. Repeat this sequence, actively thrusting the bar in one direction then the other. By flexing at the knees and keeping the torso erect, concentrate on using the torso muscles to yield to and overcome the bar's momentum.

Drill 50   **Twist Toss**

Introduction: A 9- to 15-pound medicine ball is ideal for this exercise, which works all the torso muscles involved with rotating the body. The twist toss applies to training for throwing and swinging.

Starting position: Cradle the ball next to the body at about waist level. Keep knees bent and place the feet slightly wider than the shoulders.

Action sequence: Initiate the action by rapidly twisting the torso in the direction opposite the intended toss. Abruptly check the initial action with a quick and powerful twist in the opposite direction, releasing the ball after you reach maximum torsion. Concentrate on a rapid, reactive cocking action before twisting in the direction of the throw. Use the hips as well as the shoulders and arms.

Drill 51   **Medicine Ball Scoop Throw**

Introduction: The medicine ball scoop throw is a progression of the medicine ball scoop toss. Take the extension of the torso and follow-through of the scoop motion to a point that allows the ball to travel the greatest distance behind the body.

Starting position: Assume a semisquat stance. Place the ball on the ground and between the legs, grasping it on either side. Extend the arms, hold the head up and back straight.

Action sequence: Begin by thrusting the hips forward and moving the shoulders backward while maintaining full extension of the arms. Scoop the ball backward, attempting to elevate the body and send the ball for maximum distance. Distance backward is the primary emphasis.

Drill 52　**Floor Kip**

Introduction: You need a soft, flat surface such as a wrestling mat or grass for this maneuver. The muscles of the entire torso and surrounding appendages participate in doing the floor kip. This exercise requires a high degree of coordination and explosive power in a total-body effort and is especially applicable to gymnastics, wrestling, weightlifting, and springboard diving.

Starting position: Assume a seated position with the legs together and feet dorsiflexed.

Action sequence: Keeping legs extended and together, roll backward far enough to bring the feet past the head as in a reverse somersault. At the same time, place the hands, palms down and fingers extended, on each side of the head. The body will be in a cocked configuration. To initiate the power phase, rapidly extend the legs upward and forward while pushing against the floor with the hands. Extend the hips and arms forward now, flexing the legs and bringing them under the body in anticipation of the landing. Land in a semisquat stance. Think of easing into a cocked position from the initial rollback. Concentrate on exploding upward with the entire body and, once airborne, remember to shift the hips and arms quickly forward.

Drill 53 **Horizontal Swing**

Introduction: You need a 15- to 20-pound dumbbell, kettlebell, handled medicine ball, or similar weighted object for this exercise. The drill is excellent for developing torso power and applies to baseball, golf, hockey, football, swimming, shot put, discus, and hammer throws.

Starting position: Place feet and hips square with the body in a comfortable stance. With arms extended and elbows slightly bent, hold the dumbbell at chest level with both hands at arm's length in front of the body.

Action sequence: Initiate a torquing motion by flexing the knees and pulling to one side with shoulder and arm. As momentum increases, check the motion by pulling in the opposite direction with the other shoulder and arm. Begin the checking action before the torso has swung fully in one direction; that is, use the momentum in one direction as the load (cocking action) for eliciting a plyometric response in the other direction. Allow the work to come from the shoulders and arms as well as the torso and legs.

Drill 54   **Vertical Swing**

Introduction: Use a dumbbell, kettlebell, handled medicine ball, or similar object weighing 15 to 30 pounds as in the horizontal swing. In addition to the athletic applications for the horizontal swing, the vertical swing is beneficial for weightlifting, Nordic skiing, wrestling, volleyball, and swimming.

Starting position: Grasping the dumbbell with both hands, allow it to hang at arm's length between the outstretched legs. Keep the back straight and the head up.

Action sequence: Keeping the arms extended, swing the dumbbell first in an upward, then downward motion. Resist the momentum of the dumbbell in one direction with a forceful braking effort to initiate movement in the opposite direction.

Drill 55 Leg Toss

Introduction: Equipment for this maneuver includes a 9- to 16-pound medicine ball and horizontal crossbar, chin bar, or stall bar. This exercise requires full-body involvement, affecting the entire torso and appendages. It applies to diving, football, gymnastics, and all sports involving kicking.

Starting position: One partner hangs with both hands from an appropriate bar so the feet are just touching the ground. The other partner is several feet away, ready to roll the medicine ball.

Action sequence: One partner rolls the ball in the direction of the hanging partner. As the feet contact the ball, catch it, and check its momentum with a forceful swing of the legs and flexion of the hips in the opposite direction. Concentrate on keeping the legs long and using the hips to generate most of the counterforce. The other partner retrieves the ball and repeats the sequence.

Drill 56   **Medicine Ball Scoop Toss (Multiple Response)**

Introduction: The medicine ball scoop toss is a progression of the medicine ball scoop toss that allows the ball to travel the greatest height above the body. The multiple-response version is a highly coordinated activity with a full extension and follow-through, employing a return system to quickly allow a catch-and-return sequence of repetitions.

Starting position: Assume a semisquat stance . Place the ball below the waist, grasping it on either side. Extend your arms, hold your head up and back straight.

Action sequence: Scoop the ball upward, attempting to elevate the body and send the ball for maximum height. Distance upward is the primary emphasis. As you land, ready the body to catch the ball on its return down and in front of you. Immediately upon catching the ball, do a countermovement jump and scoop the ball back up and over in the return sequence of the toss.

Drill 57 **Multiple Hops to Overhead Throw**

Introduction: This drill combines movements that work the exchange of flexion and extension motions and the subsequent hip projection in an effort as responsive and mechanically efficient as possible.

Starting position: Begin in the same position as the medicine ball scoop toss.

Action sequence: Execute a countermovement jump, then extend upward and forward for one to two yards. Upon descent, prepare the body for an overhead throw backward by positioning the hips over and slightly behind the feet. Flex the knees in readiness for extension upward and backward. Execute the throw with the least amount of ground-contact time. You can also execute this throwing motion after a series of forward hops or after one or more backward hops.

Drill 58   **Multiple Hops to Underhand Toss**

Introduction: As with the previous overhead throw, this drill combines movements that work the exchange of flexion and extension motions and the subsequent hip projection. This drill is excellent for any sports that involve quick, reactive starting movements such as track sprints; high, long, and triple jumps; football; basketball; volleyball; and others.

Starting position: Begin in the same position as the medicine ball scoop toss.

Action sequence: Begin by executing a countermovement jump, then extending upward and forward for one or two yards. Upon descent, prepare the body for an underhand shovel toss forward by positioning the hips over and slightly in front of the feet. Flex the knees in readiness for extension outward. Execute the toss with the least amount of ground-contact time. You can also execute this shoveling motion after a series of forward hops or after one or more backward hops.

UPPER BODY (Drills 59-67)

These progressive medicine ball drills are helpful to any athlete exploding from a stance, starting blocks, or off a platform (football, track, diving, etc.). The drills begin by emphasizing hip and shoulder extension and technique, then incorporate footwork and reactive work.

Table 5.2	Upper-Body Drills		
Continuum Scaling			
Low	*Moderate*	*High*	*Shock*
MB chest pass	Sit-up throw	Heavy bag stroke	
	Arm swings	Catch and overhead throw	
	Heavy bag thrust	Drop pushes	
Push or pass progression ————————>			
Overhead throw progression ————————>			
MB = medicine ball			

Drill 59 **Medicine Ball Chest Pass**

Introduction: Perform this exercise preferably with a partner (a wall can suffice), using a 7- to 15-pound medicine ball. The movement is specific to the basketball chest pass but is also beneficial in wrestling, football, and shot put.

Starting position: Partners stand, kneel, or sit facing each other. One partner holds the ball chest high with hands slightly behind the ball and arms flexed. The other partner anticipates the catch with arms extended horizontally at the chest.

Action sequence: One partner pushes the ball rapidly outward, extending arms to full length. The other partner checks the momentum of the ball and, before fully collapsing the arms, pushes outward in the opposite direction, passing it back with a full follow-through. Repeat the sequence back and forth in catch fashion.

Drill 60 **Push or Pass Progression**

Introduction: These drills are progressive variations of the medicine ball chest pass but with a push emphasis of shoulder and hip extension, rather than an elbows out triceps emphasis.

Drill 60a **Chest Push (Single Response)**

Starting position: Begin on both knees with chest out, hips high and back. Hold the ball with both hands slightly behind each side of it. Place the ball below the chest with shoulders in front and the elbows close to the body.

Action sequence: Execute the pass by exploding forward and outward with the hips while pushing the ball like a line drive as far as possible. Correct posture is critical for proper thrust and release performance. Full extension enhances execution and allows optimal time for catching the ground in push-up position.

Drill 60b **Chest Push** (Multiple Response)

Starting position: Begin in the same position as the single-response chest push.

Action sequence: Execute this exercise exactly like the single-response chest pass except that a partner or wall continues delivering the ball back to the kneeling athlete using a skip pass or bounce. After executing the same posture, thrust, extension, and follow-through, immediately resume the passing position. The partner, or wall, should aggressively skip pass the ball back into the kneeling athlete's chest. The athlete returns the bounce pass as quickly and explosively as possible by catching the ball with both hands, elbows bent, keeping the ball away from the chest and shoulders, and thrusting the hips and trunk forward.

Drill 60c Chest Push With Two- or Three-Point Stance Release

Starting position: Assume a stance specific to your activity or position. Place the ball either on the ground (for three-point positions) or hold it close to the body, in all cases directly underneath the chest.

Action sequence: Upon initiating the first step, maintain posture with the shoulders forward, chest low yet out, and head up. Grasp the ball in a position similar to the previous pass exercises. Draw the foot up underneath the body to assure that you do not overstride. Upon executing the second step, roll the hips forward to extend the trunk as you explosively release the ball like a low line drive outward. You can also perform the release with a step backward (such as in football pass blocking) rather than forward. In all cases, you must release the ball by the second step.

Drill 60d   **Chest Push With Run Release**

Starting position: Begin in the same position as the previous stance sequence.

Action sequence: Exactly as in the previous exercise, the posture and position of the first two steps allow a quick and explosive ball pass forward without overstriding. Follow the second step and synchronous ball release immediately with a sprint of 6 to 10 yards. You can incorporate these releases in many directions specific to your needs.

Drill 60e Return Push From Stance Release

(Single and Multiple Response)

Starting position: Begin in the same position as the previous stance sequence, specific to the situation. A partner is ready to initiate the throw or pass on a command signal and the athlete is in the beginning stance.

Action sequence: Upon command, the athlete releases into a posture to receive the ball, catches the ball with both hands, then explosively passes the ball like a line drive back to the partner. Multiple-response execution allows the athlete to receive the ball in a specific set-up position for several repetitions. You can extend this to movement, directional, or sprint-release situations.

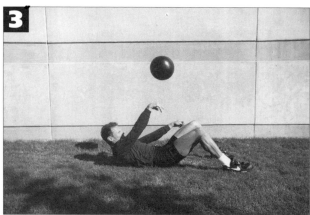

Drill 61 — Overhead Throw Progression

Introduction: Using a medicine ball to improve overall power production is extremely helpful in many areas, one of those being the overhead throwing motion in baseball, softball, football, soccer, and the javelin. Teaching and training different steps of the overhead throw progression can develop several components of this motion. You can use each step as a training phase in itself or as lead-up or warm-up activities to other throwing performances. The steps in the progression work as follows:

Drill 61a — Supine One-Arm Overhead Throw

Starting position: Lie with your back flat on the ground or a table, with feet flat and knees up.

Action sequence: Maintain a relaxed torso and long throwing arm, passing the ball forward like a line drive to a partner or against a wall. Keep the back and head relaxed and on the ground, and initiate arm movement at the shoulder joint without elbow flexion.

Drill 61b   **Supine Two-Arm Overhead Throw**

Starting position: Begin with the same ground posture and execution as in the supine one-arm overhead throw only using both arms and a larger ball (two and one-half to four kilograms).

Action sequence: Execute the pass by performing a sit-up using the momentum of the throwing motion and the thrust of chest into the desired direction. With arms long and elbows relaxed, the motion is about the shoulder joint. Lead with the chest, and follow through with flexion at the waist.

Drill 61c **Kneeling Two-Arm Overhead Throw**

Starting position: Kneel on both legs with ankles relaxed and toes back.

Action sequence: Emphasizing hip lead and follow-through, initiate the pass with a forward thrust of the hips, followed by a whipping action of the upper torso, to complete flexion at the waist upon follow-through. Keep the arms relaxed and elbows slightly flexed. Lead with the chest, and follow through with shoulders, elbows, and wrists.

Drill 61d　Standing Two-Arm Overhead Throw

Starting position:　Stand with feet together and evenly balanced.

Action sequence:　Perform the pass as in the kneeling two-arm overhead throw. Initiate the motion with knee flexion, followed by hip thrust, torso whip, and follow-through allowing for a slightly airborne body upon completion.

Drill 61e   **Stepping Two-Arm Overhead Throw**

Starting position: Use the same stance and execution as in the standing two-arm overhead throw.

Action sequence: This time initiate the movement with a lead step. You can execute this not only facing forward, but also stepping from a sideways position using rotating hip thrust and open stepping techniques. Step into the throwing direction with lead foot, hip thrust, and torso whip while pushing off with the trail leg and back foot.

Drill 62 **Sit-Up Throw**

Introduction: In this drill throw a 7- to 15-pound medicine ball to a partner or against a wall. The exercise directly stresses flexion of the upper torso and applies to all athletic activities.

Starting position: Sit on the floor facing the partner or wall with feet interlocked for stabilization. Hold the ball overhead with arms long.

Action sequence: Throw the ball with a two-hand overhand action. When you catch it on the return, the momentum forces the torso to rock backward to absorb the shock. Resist this backward motion with the abdominal muscles and initiate the return throw of the ball. Concentrate on propelling the ball with the trunk muscles, not the arms and shoulders. Aim the throw to a point above your partner's head so the arc of the throw is longer, producing greater momentum. Keep the arms extended overhead.

Drill 63   **Arm Swing**

Introduction: Use dumbbells or similar weighted handles of 10 to 40 pounds in this drill, which employs shoulder and arm muscles and simulates the alternating arm movement of cross-country skiing.

Starting position: Hold the dumbbells firmly, one in each hand. Assume a comfortable stance with feet apart and arms at the sides. Keep the head straight and tilt the shoulders slightly forward.

Action sequence: Drive one arm upward to a point just above the head while driving the other arm behind the body. Before each arm reaches maximum stretch, check the momentum by initiating motion in the opposite direction. Continue this alternating sequence for 20 to 30 swings. Perform a variation of this pattern by holding the dumbbells in a half-flexed position with the arms.

Drill 64   **Heavy Bag Thrust**

Introduction: This exercise requires a heavy punching bag suspended from a rope or cable and involves coordinating the torso and appendages in rotation and extension. The drill is well suited for discus throwers, shot-putters, football linemen, and basketball players.

Starting position: Face the punching bag with legs in a semisplit position; the foot next to the bag is back (although the reverse stance can work for some athletic positions). Place the inside hand chest high on the bag with fingers pointing upward; hold the elbow close to the body and flex the arm.

Action sequence: Keeping the feet stationary and mainly using the torso, push the bag away from the body as rapidly as possible, extending the arm and shoulder fully. Catch the return flight of the bag with open hand, and break the momentum using the trunk, arm, and shoulder muscles. Push the bag forward again before it reaches the original starting position. Concentrate on maintaining the same body stance throughout the drill. Switch sides and repeat, stressing quickness and explosiveness.

Drill 65   **Heavy Bag Stroke**

Introduction: You need a heavy punching bag suspended from a rope or cable. This drill simulates the motion of a tennis stroke but also applies to training in baseball, discus, and football.

Starting position: Assume an upright stance next to the heavy bag. Place feet slightly more than shoulder-width apart. With arm extended, rest the forearm across the bag at chest height.

Action sequence: Begin by twisting at the waist, keeping the arm extended and pushing the bag with the forearm. Continue the action until you move the bag away from the body. Catch the bag upon its return flight with the same position of the arm you used in initiating the movement. Check the momentum of the bag with the same muscle groups that initially propelled it, then powerfully reapply force in the opposite direction. Remember to follow through, rotating at the waist with each push.

Drill 66 **Catch and Overhead Throw**

Introduction: This drill demonstrates the truest sense of stretch-shortening or plyometric work for the upper body in that the reflexive response of catching stimulates all the principles of elastic-reactive training in the form of throwing.

Starting position: Begin with any of the upright starting positions in the overhead throw progression.

Action sequence: Execute an overhead throw as described in the overhead throw progressions immediately upon catching a preceding throw or rebound from a previous throw. It is important that you receive the implement in the same biomechanical position as the throwing motion for optimal safety, efficiency, and result.

Drill 67   **Drop Push**

Introduction: This drill demonstrates the truest sense of reflexive response and the principles of elastic-reactive training in the form of upper-torso pushing.

Starting position: Assume a prone position with straight torso, and extend arms from separate and elevated platforms (boxes, blocks, benches, etc.).

Action sequence: To properly progress in successful techniques, begin by dropping from the raised platforms and landing with a strictly maintained posture, cushioning the landing by giving at the shoulders and elbows.

The next progression is to perform two to four sets of a drop from the platforms, and upon landing perform a fully extended push-up. Follow this by a drop and explosive push-up, extending the torso and arms completely off the ground.

The final progression is to drop and explosively push the torso and arms back up and onto the platforms for four to eight repetitions.

Chapter 6

Sport-Specific Training

One way to take advantage of explosive training is to tailor drills to the sport you play. It not only motivates your workouts to know that your exercises will specifically help your sport, but also gives direction to the individual workouts and the progressions you plan. You should not alter the plan to progress from general to specific, from simple to complex, from low to high and shock intensity. You will see this from the workout cards that follow, the guidelines of stress sequence and of education (teaching and learning).

The following sheets provide specific plyometric workout programs using the concepts of the stress continuum. The first section offers an all-encompassing, program-basics continuum of exercises that we believe you should incorporate into the beginning of *all* plyometric training programs. Then, you will find in the following pages the 12 top sport-specific exercises, known as each sport's desirable dozens. These can accompany the program basics as you progress through weeks of the continuum. You can use the program for the full 12 weeks or any length of time. Participants and coaches can tailor the time individually or to fit the phasic constraints of the periodized training cycle (see chapter 7). For example, when we train collegiate athletes who are on the quarter system of the academic calendar, we rarely get a full 12 weeks of training without a break. Therefore, we must step back a week or two and continue accordingly to progress with the continuum. The exercise dosage we give in each column is for you to spread over two days within the week. We call these practical tables continuum cards for specific sports.

After these sport-specific drills comes a special feature for beyond basic continuum training—what we call "mountains" and "rivers." Named to depict the power, stability, and continual flow toward certain goals, we have chosen several well-known examples. These routines are advanced and appropriate for the competitive phase of training.

Continuum Training by Sport

To provide an outline of what is to come, we show these sport groupings in no particular order or ranking other than as a list of the most common activities we and our colleagues deal with regularly. If your particular sport or activity is not listed here, do not let that deter you. You know your activity, and with the guidelines in this book and the following examples, you will be able to set up your own continuum card of specific training.

- Sprinters, jumpers, and hurdlers; heptathletes and decathletes
- Throwers—for field events, quarterbacks, and pitchers
- Football linemen and backs
- Basketball
- Volleyball
- Baseball and softball
- Wrestling
- Skiing—Alpine and Nordic
- Soccer—punters and kickers
- Tennis and racquet sports
- Cycling
- Weightlifting

Twelve-Week Conditioning Program

Tables 6.1–6.14 (pp. 136–149) provide a full program of progress and development into and through specific stretch-shortening cycle training. The first 12 exercises at the top of each table are called "program basics" because they are general conditioning drills for any training program, regardless of specific sport. These basic drills are a lead-in, and the gradual steps increase in complexity and specificity as the weeks continue.

Desirable Dozens

As you look over the tables, you can see that the first few weeks consist of program basics and, in most cases, only a few sport-specific drills. We call these sport-specific drills the "desirable dozens," as they are the 12 exercises we have chosen to best apply to each sport training development. Do these desirable dozens on the same days as the program basics. Eventually some drills may take the role of technical training, or even the warm-up, but for the 12-week programming they are the training program itself. Each coach or athlete may have others to add or replace; they know their activity and can apply the principles we have discussed. For continuity, we have provided 12 such drills for basic training and specific sport work. When we give numbers, they represent the number of sets and the number of repetitions (for example, 2 sets × 4-6 repetitions). As mentioned, spread the exercises for each week over two days, preferably with one or more days of nonelastic-reactive work in between (refer to section on rest in chapter 3). You can split the workload by doing half the volume of every exercise each of the two days. However, in some cases, as with several of the third to eighth weeks, there may be 14 to 18 exercises scheduled for the week. What we have found to work well is to split the exercises into two groups, either by basics versus specifics or, even better, to split them up to match the style of training for that day. To give an example, let's say on the third week we have the 11 drills from program basics, then the 5 to 10 drills scheduled for week three in our sport-specific realm. On day one, we will do lifting and sprinting as well as the drills. On day two, we just do sprinting and the drills. In this case, we would like to choose some program basics that could fit either with the lifting (perhaps in complex style), such as pogo, squat jump, box jump, split jump, or star jump or with the sprinting, such as prancing, galloping, skipping, ankle flip, and so on. We could term this a vertical versus horizontal split in the week's drills. On the other hand, we have found it useful to split the drills by complexity or intensity, with the first several exercises of the basics and the specifics on the day that has lifting and running, and the later exercises of each section on the day with only the sprint training.

Table 6.1 — Continuum Training by Sport: Football linemen

Program Basics

Exercise	Wk1	Wk2	Wk3	Wk4	Wk5	Wk6	Wk7	Wk8	Wk9	Wk10	Wk11	Wk12
Pogo	3×10	3×10	3×10	3×10								
Squat jump	2×4-6	3×4-6	3×6-8									
Medicine ball over and under, medicine ball half and full twist	3×3	3×4	3×5	3×6	3×6							
Rocket and star jumps	2×4-6	2×4-6	3×4-6	3×4-6								
Split and scissors jumps		2×4-6	3×4-6	3×6-8	3×6-8	3×6-8	3×4-6					
Prancing	2×4-6	2×4-6	2×4-6	2×4-6	2×4-6							
Galloping	3×10	3×10	3×10	3×10	2×10	2×10	2×10	2×10	2×10	2×10	2×10	2×10
Fast skipping	3×10	3×10	3×10	3×10	2×10	2×10	2×10	2×10	2×10	2×10	2×10	2×10
Ankle flip	2×4-6	3×4-6	3×4-6	3×6-8	3×6-8	3×6-8	3×6-8	3×6-8	3×6-8	2×8-10	2×8-10	2×8-10
Single-leg stair bound		2×4-6	2×4-6	3×6-8	2×8-10	2×8-10	2×8-10		2×8-10			
Lateral bound (SR)			2×6-8	3×6-8	3×8-10	3×8-12	3×8-12	3×10-12				
Alternate leg stair bound			2×6-8	3×6-8	3×8-10	3×8-12	3×8-12	3×8-12				

Desirable Dozen

Exercise	Wk1	Wk2	Wk3	Wk4	Wk5	Wk6	Wk7	Wk8	Wk9	Wk10	Wk11	Wk12
Pit leap progression			3×4-6	3×4-6	3×6-8	3×6-8	3×6-8					
Incline ricochet			3×8-12	3×8-12	3×8-12	3×8-12	3×8-12	3×8-12	3×8-12			
Medicine ball chest pass progression				3×4-6	3×4-6	3×4-6	3×4-6	3×4-6	3×4-6			
Medicine ball scoop throw progression					3×4-6	3×4-6	3×4-6	3×4-6	3×4-6	3×4-6		
Knee-tuck jump				3×4-6	3×4-6	3×4-6	3×4-8	3×4-8	3×4-8			
Power skipping					2×4-6	3×4-6	3×4-6	4×6-8	4×6-8	4×6-8		4×8-10
Double-leg hop progression						2×4-6	3×4-6	3×4-6	3×6-8	3×6-8	3×6-8	3×6-8
Side hop-sprint								2×4-6	4×4-6	4×4-6	6×4-6	6×4-6
Side hop								3×4-6	3×6-8	3×6-8	3×6-8	3×6-8
Alternate leg bound								3×4-6	3×6-8		3×6-8	
Depth jump progression										3×3	3×3	3×3
Depth leap progression										3×3	3×3	3×3
Impact intensity		Low		Medium				High			Shock	

Table 6.2 Continuum Training by Sport: Football backs

Program Basics

Exercise / Date>	Wk1	Wk2	Wk3	Wk4	Wk5	Wk6	Wk7	Wk8	Wk9	Wk10	Wk11	Wk12
Pogo	3×10	3×10	3×10	3×10								
Squat jump	2×4-6	3×4-6	3×6-8									
Medicine ball over and under, medicine ball half and full twist	3×3	3×4	3×5	3×6	3×6							
Rocket and star jumps	2×4-6	2×4-6	3×4-6	3×4-6	3×4-6							
Split and scissors jumps			2×4-6	2×4-6	3×6-8	3×6-8	3×4-6					
Prancing	2×4-6	2×4-6	2×4-6	2×4-6	2×4-6							
Galloping	3×10	3×10	3×10	3×10	2×10	2×10	2×10	2×10	2×10	2×10	2×10	2×10
Fast skipping	3×10	3×10	3×10	3×10	2×10	2×10	2×10	2×10	2×10	2×10	2×10	2×10
Ankle flip	2×4-6	3×4-6	3×4-6	3×6-8	3×6-8	3×6-8	3×6-8	3×6-8	3×6-8	2×8-10	2×8-10	2×8-10
Single-leg stair bound		2×4-6	2×4-6	3×6-8		2×8-10	2×8-10		2×8-10			
Lateral bound (SR)			2×6-8	3×6-8	3×8-10	3×8-12		3×10-12				
Alternate leg stair bound			2×6-8	3×6-8	3×8-10	3×8-12	3×8-12	3×8-12				

Desirable Dozen

Exercise / Date>	Wk1	Wk2	Wk3	Wk4	Wk5	Wk6	Wk7	Wk8	Wk9	Wk10	Wk11	Wk12
Ricochet			3×8-12	3×8-12	3×8-12		3×8-12	3×8-12				
Knee-tuck jump			3×4-6	3×4-6	3×4-6	3×4-6	3×4-6	3×4-6	3×4-6			
Double-leg butt kick				3×4-6	3×4-6	3×4-6	3×4-6	3×4-6	3×4-6			
Double-leg hop progression					3×4-6	3×4-6	3×4-6	3×4-6	3×4-6	3×4-6		
Side hop				3×4-6	3×4-6	3×4-6	3×4-8	3×4-8				
Power skipping					2×4-6	3×4-6	3×4-6	4×6-8	4×6-8			
Alternate leg bound						2×4-6	3×4-6	3×4-6			4×8-10	3×6-8
Standing triple jump progression								2×4-6	4×4-6	4×4-6	6×4-6	6×4-6
Depth jump									4-8	4-8	4-8	4-8
Depth leap									3-6	3-6	3-6	3-6
Single-leg hop progression										2×3-6	3×3-6	3×3-6
Single-leg lateral hop progression										2×3-6	3×3-6	3×3-6
Impact intensity		Low		Medium				High			Shock	

Table 6.3 Continuum Training by Sport: Track (sprint, jump, hurdle)

Program Basics

Exercise Date>	Wk1	Wk2	Wk3	Wk4	Wk5	Wk6	Wk7	Wk8	Wk9	Wk10	Wk11	Wk12
Pogo	3×10	3×10	3×10	3×10								
Squat jump	2×4-6	3×4-6	3×6-8									
Medicine ball over and under, medicine ball half and full twist	3×3	3×4	3×5	3×6	3×6							
Rocket and star jumps	2×4-6	2×4-6	3×4-6		3×4-6							
Split and scissors jumps	2×4-6	2×4-6	3×6-8		3×6-8	3×6-8	3×4-6					
Prancing	2×4-6	2×4-6	2×4-6	2×4-6	2×4-6							
Galloping	3×10	3×10	3×10	3×10	2×10	2×10	2×10	2×10	2×10	2×10	2×10	2×10
Fast skipping	3×10	3×10	3×10	3×10	2×10	2×10	2×10	2×10	2×10	2×10	2×10	2×10
Ankle flip	2×4-6	3×4-6	3×4-6	3×6-8	3×6-8	3×6-8	3×6-8	3×6-8	3×6-8	2×8-10	2×8-10	2×8-10
Single-leg stair bound		2×4-6	2×4-6	3×6-8	2×8-10	2×8-10	2×8-10		2×8-10			
Lateral bound (SR)			2×6-8	3×6-8	3×8-10	3×8-12	3×8-12	3×10-12				
Alternate leg stair bound			2×6-8	3×6-8	3×8-10	3×8-12	3×8-12	3×8-12				

Desirable Dozen

Exercise Date>	Wk1	Wk2	Wk3	Wk4	Wk5	Wk6	Wk7	Wk8	Wk9	Wk10	Wk11	Wk12
Knee-tuck jump		3×4-6	3×4-6	3×4-6	3×6-8	3×6-8						
Single-leg stride jump			3×4	3×5	3×6	3×6	3×6	3×6				
Alternate leg bound					3×6-8	3×8-10	3×8-12	3×8-12	3×10+	3×10-12		
Double-leg butt kick					3×6-8	3×6-8	3×8-10	3×8-10	3×8-10	3×8-10	3×8-10	3×8-10
Single-leg hop progression				3×3	3×4	3×5	3×6	3×6	3×6	3×6	3×6	3×6
Hurdle hop					2×4-6	3×6-8	3×6-8	4×6-8	4×6-8	4×6-8	4×6-8	4×6-8
Side hop					2×4-6	2×4-6	3×4-6	3×4-6	3×6-8	3×6-8	3×6-8	3×6-8
Single-leg hop progression								2×3	3×3	3×3-5	3×5-7	3×6-8
Depth jump progression									1×3	1×4	1×5	1×7
Combination jumps and bounds										3×3	3×3	3×3
Jumps and hops decathlon											2×2	
Box bound											3×3	3×3
Impact intensity		Low		Medium				High			Shock	

Table 6.4 Continuum Training by Sport: Throwers (field events, quarterbacks, pitchers)

Program Basics

Exercise (Date>)	Wk1	Wk2	Wk3	Wk4	Wk5	Wk6	Wk7	Wk8	Wk9	Wk10	Wk11	Wk12
Pogo	3×10	3×10	3×10	3×10								
Squat jump	2×4-6	3×4-6	3×6-8									
Medicine ball over and under, medicine ball half and full twist	3×3	3×4	3×5	3×6	3×6							
Rocket and star jumps	2×4-6	2×4-6	3×4-6	3×4-6	3×4-6							
Split and scissors jumps		2×4-6		3×4-6	3×6-8	3×6-8	3×4-6					
Prancing	2×4-6	2×4-6	2×4-6	2×4-6	2×4-6							
Galloping	3×10	3×10	3×10	3×10	2×10	2×10	2×10	2×10	2×10	2×10	2×10	2×10
Fast skipping	3×10	3×10	3×10	3×10	2×10	2×10	2×10	2×10	2×10	2×10	2×10	2×10
Ankle flip	2×4-6	3×4-6	3×4-6	3×6-8	3×6-8	3×6-8	3×6-8	3×6-8	3×6-8	2×8-10	2×8-10	2×8-10
Single-leg stair bound		2×4-6	2×4-6	3×6-8	2×8-10	2×8-10	2×8-10		2×8-10			
Lateral bound (SR)			2×6-8	3×6-8	3×8-10	3×8-12		3×10-12				
Alternate leg stair bound			2×6-8	3×6-8	3×8-10	3×8-12	3×8-12	3×8-12				

Desirable Dozen

Exercise (Date>)	Wk1	Wk2	Wk3	Wk4	Wk5	Wk6	Wk7	Wk8	Wk9	Wk10	Wk11	Wk12
Ricochet	3×8-12	3×8-12	3×8-12	3×8-12	3×8-12	3×8-12						
Bar twist	3×8-12	3×8-12	3×8-12	3×8-12	3×8-12	3×8-12	3×8-12					
Twist toss progression	3×12-20		3×12-20	3×12-20		3×12-20	3×12-20					
Heavy bag thrust		3×4-6	3×4-6	3×4-6	3×4-6	3×4-6	3×4-6					
Heavy bag stroke		3×6-12	3×6-12	3×6-12	3×6-12	3×6-12						
Shovel toss		3×4-6	3×4-6	3×6-8	3×6-8		3×8-10	3×8-10				
Medicine ball scoop toss progression				3×4-6		3×4-6		3×6-8	3×6-8		3×6-8	
Medicine ball scoop throw progression					3×4-6	3×4-6	3×4-6	3×6-8		3×6-8		3×6-8
Forward throw progression			2×4-6	2×4-6	3×4-6	3×4-6	3×4-6		3×6-8	3×6-8	3×6-8	3×6-8
Sit-up throw progression			2×10-20	2×10-20		2×10-20		2×10-20	2×10-20	2×10-20	2×10-20	2×10-20
Horizontal swing						2×8-12	2×8-12	2×8-12	2×8-12		2×8-12	2×8-12
Floor kip					2×3-6		2×3-6	2×3-6	3×3-6	3×3-6	3×3-6	3×3-6
Impact intensity		Low		Medium				High			Shock	

Table 6.5 — Continuum Training by Sport: Basketball, Netball

Program Basics

Exercise / Date>	Wk1	Wk2	Wk3	Wk4	Wk5	Wk6	Wk7	Wk8	Wk9	Wk10	Wk11	Wk12
Pogo	3×10	3×10	3×10	3×10								
Squat jump	2×4-6	3×4-6	3×6-8									
Medicine ball over and under, medicine ball half and full twist	3×3	3×4	3×5	3×6	3×6							
Rocket and star jumps	2×4-6	2×4-6	3×4-6	3×4-6	3×4-6							
Split and scissors jumps		2×4-6		3×6-8	3×6-8	3×6-8	3×4-6					
Prancing	2×4-6	2×4-6	2×4-6	2×4-6	2×4-6							
Galloping	3×10	3×10	3×10	3×10	2×10	2×10	2×10	2×10	2×10	2×10	2×10	2×10
Fast skipping	3×10	3×10	3×10	3×10	2×10	2×10	2×10	2×10	2×10	2×10	2×10	2×10
Ankle flip	2×4-6	3×4-6	3×4-6	3×6-8	3×6-8	3×6-8	3×6-8	3×6-8	3×6-8	2×8-10	2×8-10	2×8-10
Single-leg stair bound		2×4-6	2×4-6	3×6-8	2×8-10	2×8-10	2×8-10		2×8-10			
Lateral bound (SR)			2×6-8	3×6-8	3×8-10	3×8-12		3×10-12				
Alternate leg stair bound			2×6-8	3×6-8	3×8-10	3×8-12	3×8-12	3×8-12				

Desirable Dozen

Exercise / Date>	Wk1	Wk2	Wk3	Wk4	Wk5	Wk6	Wk7	Wk8	Wk9	Wk10	Wk11	Wk12
Medicine ball scoop toss progression	2×4-6	2×4-6	2×4-6									
Medicine ball twist toss			3×8-12	3×8-12	3×8-12	3×8-12	3×8-12	3×8-12				
Medicine ball pass progression			3×4-6	3×4-6	3×4-6	3×4-6	3×4-6	3×4-6	3×4-6			
Medicine ball sit-up throw				3×4-6	3×4-6	3×4-6	3×4-6	3×4-6	3×4-6			
Lateral bound					3×4-6	3×4-6	3×4-6	3×4-6	3×4-6	3×4-6		
Ricochet				3×4-6	3×4-6	3×4-6	3×4-8	3×4-8				
Double-leg hop progression								4×6-8	4×6-8		4×8-10	
Side hop					2×4-6		3×4-6	3×4-6		3×6-8	3×6-8	3×6-8
Incremental vertical hop								2×4-6	4×4-6	4×4-6	6×4-6	6×4-6
Side hop-sprint									4-8	4-8	4-8	4-8
Drop-sprint									3-6	3-6	3-6	3-6
Depth jump progression										2×3-6	3×3-6	3×3-6
Impact intensity		Low		Medium				High			Shock	

Table 6.6 — Continuum Training by Sport: Volleyball

Program Basics

Exercise Date>	Wk1	Wk2	Wk3	Wk4	Wk5	Wk6	Wk7	Wk8	Wk9	Wk10	Wk11	Wk12
Pogo	3×10	3×10	3×10	3×10								
Squat jump	2×4-6	3×4-6	3×6-8									
Medicine ball over and under, medicine ball half and full twist	3×3	3×4	3×5	3×6	3×6							
Rocket and star jumps	2×4-6	2×4-6	3×4-6									
Split and scissors jumps			2×4-6	3×4-6	3×6-8	3×6-8	3×4-6					
Prancing	2×4-6	2×4-6	2×4-6	2×4-6	2×4-6							
Galloping	3×10	3×10	3×10	3×10	2×10	2×10	2×10	2×10	2×10	2×10	2×10	2×10
Fast skipping	3×10	3×10	3×10	3×10	2×10	2×10	2×10	2×10	2×10	2×10	2×10	2×10
Ankle flip	2×4-6	3×4-6	3×4-6	3×6-8	3×6-8	3×6-8	3×6-8	3×6-8	3×6-8	2×8-10	2×8-10	2×8-10
Single-leg stair bound		2×4-6	2×4-6	3×6-8	2×8-10	2×8-10	2×8-10	3×10-12	2×8-10			
Lateral bound (SR)			2×6-8	3×6-8	3×8-10	3×8-12	3×8-12	3×8-12				
Alternate leg stair bound			2×6-8	3×6-8	3×8-10	3×8-12	3×8-12	3×8-12				

Desirable Dozen

Exercise Date>	Wk1	Wk2	Wk3	Wk4	Wk5	Wk6	Wk7	Wk8	Wk9	Wk10	Wk11	Wk12
Shovel toss	2×4-6	2×4-6	2×4-6									
Twist toss			3×8-12	3×8-12	3×8-12	3×8-12	3×8-12	3×8-12				
Sit-up throw			3×12-20	3×12-20	3×12-20	3×12-20	3×12-20	3×12-20	3×12-20			
Overhead throw progression				3×4-6	3×4-6	3×4-6	3×4-6	3×4-6	3×4-6			
Ricochet		3×4-6	3×4-6	3×4-6	3×6-12	3×6-12	3×6-12	3×6-12				
Lateral bound-net jumps		3×4-6	3×4-6	3×4-6	3×4-6	3×4-8	3×4-8	3×4-8				
Power skipping			2×4-6	2×4-6	2×4-6	3×4-6	3×4-6	4×6-8	4×6-8		4×8-10	
Side hop					2×4-6	2×4-6	3×4-6	3×4-6		3×6-8		3×6-8
Incremental vertical hop					2×4-6	2×4-6	3×4-6		3×6-8	3×6-8	3×6-8	3×6-8
Side hop-sprint						2×4-6	2×4-6		2×4-6	2×4-6	2×4-6	2×4-6
Drop-sprint						2-4×2	3-6×2	3-6×2	3-6×2		3-6×2	3-6×2
Depth jump progression										2×3-6	3×3-6	3×3-6
Impact intensity		Low		Medium				High			Shock	

Table 6.7 Continuum Training by Sport: Baseball, Softball, Cricket

Program Basics

Exercise Date>	Wk1	Wk2	Wk3	Wk4	Wk5	Wk6	Wk7	Wk8	Wk9	Wk10	Wk11	Wk12
Pogo	3×10	3×10	3×10	3×10								
Squat jump	2×4-6	3×4-6	3×6-8									
Medicine ball over and under, medicine ball half and full twist	3×3	3×4	3×5	3×6	3×6							
Rocket and star jumps	2×4-6	2×4-6	3×4-6	3×4-6	3×4-6	3×6-8						
Split and scissors jumps	2×4-6	2×4-6		2×4-6	3×6-8		3×4-6					
Prancing	2×4-6	2×4-6	2×4-6	2×4-6	2×4-6							
Galloping	3×10	3×10	3×10	3×10	2×10	2×10	2×10	2×10	2×10	2×10	2×10	2×10
Fast skipping	3×10	3×10	3×10	3×10	2×10	2×10	2×10	2×10	2×10	2×10	2×10	2×10
Ankle flip	2×4-6	3×4-6	3×4-6	3×6-8	3×6-8	3×6-8	3×6-8	3×6-8	3×6-8	2×8-10	2×8-10	2×8-10
Single-leg stair bound (SR)		2×4-6	2×4-6	3×6-8	3×8-10	2×8-10	2×8-10		2×8-10			
Lateral bound (SR)			2×6-8	3×6-8	3×8-10	3×8-12	3×8-12	3×10-12				
Alternate leg stair bound			2×6-8	3×6-8	3×8-10	3×8-12	3×8-12	3×8-12				

Desirable Dozen

Exercise	Wk1	Wk2	Wk3	Wk4	Wk5	Wk6	Wk7	Wk8	Wk9	Wk10	Wk11	Wk12
Bar twist	3×8-12	3×8-12	3×8-12	3×8-12	3×8-12	3×8-12						
Heavy bag stroke		3×8-12	3×8-12	3×8-12	3×8-12		3×8-12	3×8-12				
Sit-up throws		3×12-20	3×12-20	3×12-20		3×12-20	3×12-20		3×12-20			
Medicine ball scoop throw progression				3×4-6	3×4-6	3×4-6	3×4-6	3×4-6	3×4-6			
Twist toss progression		3×6-12	3×6-12	3×6-12		3×6-12	3×6-12					
Horizontal swing		3×4-6	3×4-6	3×6-8	3×6-8		3×8-10	3×8-10				
Incline ricochet		2×6-10	2×6-10	2×6-10	2×6-10	3×6-12		3×6-12	3×6-12		3×6-12	
Knee-tuck jump			2×4-6		3×4-6	3×4-6	3×4-6	3×6-8		3×6-8		3×6-8
Double-leg butt kick				2×4-6	3×4-6	3×4-6	3×4-6		3×6-8	3×6-8	3×6-8	3×6-8
Power skipping		2×4-6	2×4-6	2×4-6		2×4-6	2×4-6		2×4-6	2×4-6	2×4-6	2×4-6
Double-leg hop progression						2-4×2	3-6×2	3-6×2	3-6×2		3-6×2	3-6×2
Side hop					2×3-6		2×3-6	2×3-6	3×3-6	3×3-6	3×3-6	3×3-6
Impact intensity		Low		Medium				High			Shock	

Table 6.8 Continuum Training by Sport: Wrestling

Program Basics

Exercise Date>	Wk1	Wk2	Wk3	Wk4	Wk5	Wk6	Wk7	Wk8	Wk9	Wk10	Wk11	Wk12
Pogo	3×10	3×10	3×10	3×10								
Squat jump	2×4-6	3×4-6	3×6-8									
Medicine ball over and under, medicine ball half and full twist	3×3	3×4	3×5	3×6	3×6							
Rocket and star jumps	2×4-6	2×4-6	3×4-6		3×4-6							
Split and scissors jumps		2×4-6	2×4-6	3×4-6	3×6-8	3×6-8						
Prancing	2×4-6	2×4-6	2×4-6	2×4-6	2×4-6							
Galloping	3×10	3×10	3×10	3×10	2×10	2×10	2×10	2×10	2×10	2×10	2×10	2×10
Fast skipping	3×10	3×10	3×10	3×10	2×10	2×10	2×10	2×10	2×10	2×10	2×10	2×10
Ankle flip	2×4-6	3×4-6	3×4-6	3×6-8	3×6-8	3×6-8	3×6-8	3×6-8	3×6-8	2×8-10	2×8-10	2×8-10
Single-leg stair bound		2×4-6	2×4-6	3×6-8	2×8-10	2×8-10	2×8-10		2×8-10			
Lateral bound (SR)			2×6-8	3×6-8	3×8-10	3×8-12		3×10-12				
Alternate leg stair bound			2×6-8	3×6-8	3×8-10	3×8-12	3×8-12	3×8-12				

Desirable Dozen

Exercise Date>	Wk1	Wk2	Wk3	Wk4	Wk5	Wk6	Wk7	Wk8	Wk9	Wk10	Wk11	Wk12
Bar twist	3×8-12	3×8-12	3×8-12	3×8-12	3×8-12	3×8-12						
Medicine ball scoop toss progression			3×8-12	3×8-12	3×8-12		3×8-12	3×8-12				
Medicine ball scoop throw progression			3×12-20	3×12-20		3×12-20	3×12-20		3×12-20			
Knee-tuck jump				3×4-6	3×4-6	3×4-6	3×4-6	3×4-6	3×4-6			
Power skipping		3×6-12	3×6-12	3×6-12		3×6-12	3×6-12					
Single-leg stride jump		3×4-6	3×4-6		3×6-8	3×6-8	3×8-10	3×8-10				
Floor kip			2×6-10	2×6-10	2×6-10	3×6-12		3×6-12	3×6-12		3×6-12	
Horizontal and vertical swings								3×6-8		3×6-8		3×6-8
Leap progression			2×4-6	2×4-6	3×4-6	3×4-6	3×4-6		3×6-8	3×6-8	3×6-8	3×6-8
Side hop			2×4-6	2×4-6		2×4-6	2×4-6		2×4-6	2×4-6	2×4-6	2×4-6
Single-leg hop progression							2×3-6	2×3-6	2×3-6	2-3×3-6	3-4×3-6	4×3-6
Single-leg diagonal hop								2×3-6	3×3-6	3×3-6	3×3-6	3×3-6
Impact intensity		Low		Medium				High			Shock	

Table 6.9   Continuum Training by Sport: Skiing (Alpine)

Program Basics

Exercise Date>	Wk1	Wk2	Wk3	Wk4	Wk5	Wk6	Wk7	Wk8	Wk9	Wk10	Wk11	Wk12
Pogo	3×10	3×10	3×10	3×10								
Squat jump	2×4-6	3×4-6	3×6-8									
Medicine ball over and under, medicine ball half and full twist	3×3	3×4	3×5	3×6	3×6							
Rocket and star jumps	2×4-6	2×4-6	3×4-6	3×4-6	3×4-6							
Split and scissors jumps		2×4-6			3×6-8	3×6-8	3×4-6					
Prancing	2×4-6	2×4-6	2×4-6	2×4-6	2×4-6							
Galloping	3×10	3×10	3×10	3×10	2×10	2×10	2×10	2×10	2×10	2×10	2×10	2×10
Fast skipping	3×10	3×10	3×10	3×10	2×10	2×10	2×10	2×10	2×10	2×10	2×10	2×10
Ankle flip	2×4-6	3×4-6	3×4-6	3×6-8	3×6-8	3×6-8	3×6-8	3×6-8	3×6-8	2×8-10	2×8-10	2×8-10
Single-leg stair bound		2×4-6	2×4-6	3×6-8	2×8-10	2×8-10	2×8-10		2×8-10			
Lateral bound (SR)			2×6-8	3×6-8	3×8-10	3×8-12		3×10-12				
Alternate leg stair bound			2×6-8	3×6-8	3×8-10	3×8-12	3×8-12	3×8-12				

Desirable Dozen

Exercise	Wk1	Wk2	Wk3	Wk4	Wk5	Wk6	Wk7	Wk8	Wk9	Wk10	Wk11	Wk12
Ricochet			3×8-12	3×8-12	3×8-12		3×8-12	3×8-12				
Knee-tuck jump			3×4-6	3×4-6	3×4-6	3×4-6	3×4-6	3×4-6	3×4-6			
Single-leg stride jump				3×4-6	3×4-6	3×4-6	3×4-6	3×4-6	3×4-6			
Stride jump crossover					3×4-6	3×4-6	3×4-6	3×4-6	3×4-6	3×4-6		
Quick leap				3×4-6	3×4-6	3×4-6	3×4-8	3×4-8				
Double-leg incline and stair bound								4×6-8	4×6-8		4×8-10	
Alternate leg bound					2×4-6	2×4-6	3×4-6	3×6-8		3×8-12		3×8-12
Double-leg hop progression								2×4-6	3×6-8	3×6-8	3×6-10	3×6-10
Side hop									2×4-6	3×4-6	3×4-6	3×4-6
Incremental vertical hop												
Single-leg hop progression									2×3-6	2×3-6	4×3-6	4×3-6
Single-leg diagonal hop										2×3-6	4×3-6	4×3-6
Impact intensity		Low		Medium				High			Shock	

Table 6.10 — Continuum Training by Sport: Skiing (Nordic)

Program Basics

Exercise	Wk1	Wk2	Wk3	Wk4	Wk5	Wk6	Wk7	Wk8	Wk9	Wk10	Wk11	Wk12
Pogo	3×10	3×10	3×10	3×10								
Squat jump	2×4-6	3×4-6	3×6-8									
Medicine ball over and under, medicine ball half and full twist	3×3	3×4	3×5	3×6	3×6							
Rocket and star jumps	2×4-6	2×4-6	3×4-6		3×4-6							
Split and scissors jumps		2×4-6		3×4-6	3×6-8	3×6-8	3×4-6					
Prancing	2×4-6	2×4-6	2×4-6	2×4-6	2×4-6							
Galloping	3×10	3×10	3×10	3×10	2×10	2×10	2×10	2×10	2×10	2×10	2×10	2×10
Fast skipping	3×10	3×10	3×10	3×10	2×10	2×10	2×10	2×10	2×10	2×10	2×10	2×10
Ankle flip	2×4-6	3×4-6	3×4-6	3×6-8	3×6-8	3×6-8	3×6-8	3×6-8	3×6-8	2×8-10	2×8-10	2×8-10
Single-leg stair bound		2×4-6	2×4-6	3×6-8		2×8-10	2×8-10		2×8-10			
Lateral bound (SR)			2×6-8	3×6-8	3×8-10	3×8-12	3×8-12	3×10-12				
Alternate leg stair bound			2×6-8	3×6-8	3×8-10	3×8-12	3×8-12	3×8-12				

Desirable Dozen

Exercise	Wk1	Wk2	Wk3	Wk4	Wk5	Wk6	Wk7	Wk8	Wk9	Wk10	Wk11	Wk12
Sit-up throw progression	2×3-6	3×3-6	3×5-8	3×6-12	3×6-12	3×6-12						
Vertical swing		3×6-12	3×6-12	3×6-12	3×6-12	3×6-12	3×6-12					
Arm swing			3×6-12	3×6-12	3×6-12	3×6-12	3×6-12	3×6-12	3×6-12			
Ricochet			3×8-12	3×8-12	3×8-12		3×8-12	3×8-12				
Knee-tuck jump			3×4-6	3×4-6	3×4-6	3×4-6	3×4-6	3×4-6	3×4-6			
Single-leg stride jump				3×4-6	3×4-6	3×4-6	3×4-6	3×4-6	3×4-6			
Stride jump crossover					3×4-6	3×4-6	3×4-6	3×4-6	3×4-6	3×4-6		
Quick leap				3×4-6	3×4-6	3×4-6	3×4-8	3×4-8				
Double-leg incline and stair bound						3×4-6	3×4-6	4×6-8	4×6-8		4×8-10	
Alternate leg bound					2×4-6	2×4-6	3×6-8	3×6-8		3×8-12		3×8-12
Single-leg hop progression										2×3-6	4×3-6	4×3-6
Single-leg diagonal hop										2×3-6	4×3-6	4×3-6
Impact intensity		Low		Medium				High			Shock	

Table 6.11   Continuum Training by Sport: Soccer, Football (punters, kickers), Lacrosse, Field Hockey, Aussie Football

Program Basics

Exercise Date>	Wk1	Wk2	Wk3	Wk4	Wk5	Wk6	Wk7	Wk8	Wk9	Wk10	Wk11	Wk12
Pogo	3×10	3×10	3×10	3×10								
Squat jump	2×4-6	3×4-6	3×6-8									
Medicine ball over and under, medicine ball half and full twist	3×3	3×4	3×5	3×6	3×6							
Rocket and star jumps	2×4-6	2×4-6	3×4-6	3×4-6	3×4-6							
Split and scissors jumps		2×4-6		3×4-6	3×6-8	3×6-8	3×4-6					
Prancing	2×4-6	2×4-6	2×4-6	2×4-6	2×4-6							
Galloping	3×10	3×10	3×10	3×10	2×10	2×10	2×10	2×10	2×10	2×10	2×10	2×10
Fast skipping	3×10	3×10	3×10	3×10	2×10	2×10	2×10	2×10	2×10	2×10	2×10	2×10
Ankle flip	2×4-6	3×4-6	3×4-6	3×6-8	3×6-8	3×6-8	3×6-8	3×6-8	3×6-8	2×8-10	2×8-10	2×8-10
Single-leg stair bound		2×4-6	2×4-6	3×6-8	3×8-10	2×8-10	2×8-10		2×8-10			
Lateral bound (SR)					3×8-10	3×8-12		3×10-12				
Alternate leg stair bound			2×6-8	3×6-8	3×8-10	3×8-12	3×8-12	3×8-12				

Desirable Dozen

Exercise Date>	Wk1	Wk2	Wk3	Wk4	Wk5	Wk6	Wk7	Wk8	Wk9	Wk10	Wk11	Wk12
Ricochet			3×8-12	3×8-12	3×8-12		3×8-12	3×8-12				
Knee-tuck jump			3×4-6	3×4-6	3×4-6	3×4-6	3×4-6	3×4-6	3×4-6			
Single-leg stride jump				3×4-6	3×4-6	3×4-6	3×4-6	3×4-6	3×4-6			
Stride jump crossover					3×4-6	3×4-6	3×4-6	3×4-6	3×4-6	3×4-6		
Power skipping				3×4-6	3×4-6	3×4-6	3×4-8	3×4-8				
Alternate leg bound					2×4-6	3×4-6	3×4-6	3×6-8	3×8-10		3×8-12	
Incremental vertical hop						2×4-6	3×4-6					
Side hop								2×4-6	3×6-8	3×6-8	3×6-10	3×6-10
Single-leg hop progression									2×4-6	3×4-6	3×4-6	3×4-6
Single-leg diagonal hop									2×3-6	3×3-6	3×3-6	3×3-6
Leg toss										2×3-6	4×3-6	4×3-6
Medicine ball overhead throw forward										2×3-6	4×3-6	4×3-6
Impact intensity		Low		Medium				High			Shock	

Table 6.12   Continuum Training by Sport: Tennis, Racquetball, Squash, Handball

Program Basics

Exercise Date>	Wk1	Wk2	Wk3	Wk4	Wk5	Wk6	Wk7	Wk8	Wk9	Wk10	Wk11	Wk12
Pogo	3×10	3×10	3×10	3×10								
Squat jump	2×4-6	3×4-6	3×6-8									
Medicine ball over and under, medicine ball half and full twist	3×3	3×4	3×5	3×6	3×6							
Rocket and star jumps	2×4-6	2×4-6	3×4-6		3×4-6							
Split and scissors jumps		2×4-6	2×4-6	3×4-6	3×6-8	3×6-8	3×4-6					
Prancing	2×4-6	2×4-6	2×4-6	2×4-6	2×4-6							
Galloping	3×10	3×10	3×10	3×10	2×10	2×10	2×10	2×10	2×10	2×10	2×10	2×10
Fast skipping	3×10	3×10	3×10	3×10	2×10	2×10	2×10	2×10	2×10	2×10	2×10	2×10
Ankle flip	2×4-6	3×4-6	3×4-6	3×6-8	3×6-8	3×6-8	3×6-8	3×6-8	3×6-8	2×8-10	2×8-10	2×8-10
Single-leg stair bound		2×4-6	2×4-6	3×6-8	3×6-8	2×8-10	2×8-10		2×8-10			
Lateral bound (SR)			2×6-8	3×6-8	3×8-10	3×8-12	3×8-12	3×10-12				
Alternate leg stair bound			2×6-8	3×6-8	3×8-10	3×8-12	3×8-12	3×8-12				

Desirable Dozen

Exercise	Wk1	Wk2	Wk3	Wk4	Wk5	Wk6	Wk7	Wk8	Wk9	Wk10	Wk11	Wk12
Overhead throw progression		2×3-6	2×3-6	2×3-6	2×3-6		2×3-6	2×3-6				
Twist toss			3×4-6	3×4-6	3×4-6	3×4-6	3×4-6	3×4-6	3×4-6			
Stride jump crossover				3×4-6	3×4-6	3×4-6	3×4-6	3×4-6	3×4-6			
Heavy bag stroke					3×4-6	3×4-6	3×4-6	3×4-6	3×4-6	3×4-6		
Horizontal swing				2×4-6	2×4-6	3×4-6	3×4-8	3×6-10				
Single-leg hop progression					2×4-6	3×4-6	3×4-6	3×6-8	3×8-10		3×8-12	
Side hop						2×4-6	3×4-6	3×6-8		3×6-8		3×6-8
Side hop-sprint								2×4-6	3×4-6	3×4-6	3×4-6	3×4-6
Lateral bound (MR)									2×4-6	3×4-6	3×4-6	3×4-6
Single-leg hop progression									2×3-6	3×3-6	3×3-6	3×3-6
Single-leg diagonal hop										2×3-6	2×3-6	2×3-6
Hop-throw and toss									2×3-6		2×3-6	2×3-6
Impact intensity		Low		Medium				High			Shock	

Table 6.13 Continuum Training by Sport: Cycling (road, criterium, track)

Program Basics

Exercise Date>	Wk1	Wk2	Wk3	Wk4	Wk5	Wk6	Wk7	Wk8	Wk9	Wk10	Wk11	Wk12
Pogo	3×10	3×10	3×10	3×10								
Squat jump	2×4-6	3×4-6	3×6-8									
Medicine ball over and under, medicine ball half and full twist	3×3	3×4	3×5	3×6	3×6							
Rocket and star jumps	2×4-6	2×4-6	3×4-6	3×4-6	3×4-6							
Split and scissors jumps					3×6-8	3×6-8	3×4-6					
Prancing	2×4-6	2×4-6	2×4-6	2×4-6	2×4-6							
Galloping	3×10	3×10	3×10	3×10	2×10	2×10	2×10	2×10	2×10	2×10	2×10	2×10
Fast skipping	3×10	3×10	3×10	3×10	2×10	2×10	2×10	2×10	2×10	2×10	2×10	2×10
Ankle flip	2×4-6	3×4-6	3×4-6	3×6-8	3×6-8	3×6-8	3×6-8	3×6-8	3×6-8	2×8-10	2×8-10	2×8-10
Single-leg stair bound		2×4-6	2×4-6	3×6-8	3×8-10	2×8-10	2×8-10		2×8-10			
Lateral bound (SR)			2×6-8	3×6-8	3×8-12	3×8-12		3×10-12				
Alternate leg stair bound			2×6-8	3×6-8	3×8-10	3×8-12	3×8-12	3×8-12				
Ricochet		2×6-10	2×6-10	2×6-10		2×6-10	2×6-10	2×6-10				
Knee-tuck jump			3×4-6	3×4-6	3×4-6		3×4-6	3×4-6	3×4-6			
Single-leg stride jump				3×4-6	3×4-6	3×4-6		3×4-6	3×4-6	3×4-6		
Stride jump crossover							3×6-8	3×6-8	3×6-8	3×6-8	3×6-8	3×6-8
Double-leg hop progression					2×4-8	3×4-8	3×6-8	3×6-8	3×6-10	3×6-12	3×6-1	3×6-1
Alternate leg bound					2×6-8	2×6-8		3×6-8		3×6-10	3×6-1	3×6-1
Single-leg hop progression							2×4-6	2×4-6	2×4-8		4×4-8	4×4-8
Depth jump										4-6×3	4-6×3	4-6×3
Impact intensity	Low			Medium				High			Shock	

Table 6.14 — Continuum Training by Sport: Weight lifting (Olympic)

Program Basics

Exercise Date>	Wk1	Wk2	Wk3	Wk4	Wk5	Wk6	Wk7	Wk8	Wk9	Wk10	Wk11	Wk12
Pogo	3×10	3×10	3×10	3×10								
Squat jump	2×4-6	3×4-6	3×6-8									
Medicine ball over and under, medicine ball half and full twist	3×3	3×4	3×5	3×6	3×6							
Rocket and star jumps	2×4-6	2×4-6	3×4-6		3×4-6							
Split and scissors jumps		2×4-6	2×4-6	3×4-6	3×6-8	3×6-8	3×4-6					
Prancing	2×4-6	2×4-6	2×4-6	2×4-6	2×4-6							
Galloping	3×10	3×10	3×10	3×10	2×10	2×10	2×10	2×10	2×10	2×10	2×10	2×10
Fast skipping	3×10	3×10	3×10	3×10	2×10	2×10	2×10	2×10	2×10	2×10	2×10	2×10
Ankle flip	2×4-6	3×4-6	3×4-6	3×6-8	3×6-8	3×6-8	3×6-8	3×6-8	3×6-8	2×8-10	2×8-10	2×8-10
Single-leg stair bound		2×4-6	2×4-6	3×6-8	3×8-10	2×8-10	2×8-10	3×10-12	2×8-10			
Lateral bound (SR)				3×6-8	3×8-10	3×8-12	3×8-12	3×8-12				
Alternate leg stair bound			2×6-8	3×6-8	3×8-10	3×8-12	3×8-12	3×8-12				
Medicine ball scoop toss progression			3×3-6	3×3-6	3×3-6		3×3-6	3×3-6	3×3-6			
Knee-tuck jump			3×3-6	3×3-6	3×3-6		3×3-6	3×3-6	3×3-6			
Incremental vertical hop				3×3-6	3×3-6	3×3-6		3×3-6	3×3-6	3×3-6		
Quick leap				4-8×1-2	4-8×1-2	4-8×1-2	4-8×1-2		4-8×1-2	4-8×1-2	4-8×1-2	4-8×1-2
Floor kip					3×1	3×1	3×1	3×1	3×1	3×1	3×1	3×1
Depth jump									4-8×3-6	4-8×3-6	4-8×3-6	4-8×3-6
Depth jump leap										3-6×3-5	3-6×3-5	3-6×3-5
Impact intensity		Low		Medium				High			Shock	

Mountains and Rivers

Once you have performed the program basics, then the specific desirable exercises as they pertain to the sport's activities, you can assign different routines to certain days on a weekly or biweekly basis. These multiple plyometric routines of jumps, bounds, hops, and throws are advanced due to dosages and intensities, but do not necessarily have to be high or shock stress.

The mountain and river routines (see below) fit best into the advanced or competitive phase of training. (We call these routines "mountains and rivers" for convenience in referring to them by name—you might prefer personalizing them, perhaps naming them after your favorite athletes, or if you're a coach, you might name them after your former favorite students. In any case, you should probably not advance into the mountain and river routines until you have accomplished all the progressions, initially, rehabilitatively, and transitionally (from the end of the competitive season into the next preparational season). As we will detail in chapter 7, you can progress into and out of different levels of stretch-shortening cycle training during phases of the precompetitive and competitive periods in several ways. Working into cycled variations of the mountain and river routines are examples of employing specific exercises and areas of development that best fit the specificity and designs of a particular competitive training period.

You can set up your own series of mountains and rivers, basing it on the past accomplishments, particular needs, and future goals and objectives of the competitive training period.

Mountain and River Routines

Mt. Everest: Stairs

1. Double-leg bound
2. Stair skip
3. Single-leg bound
4. Lateral bound
5. Alternate leg bound
6. Ricochet

Mississippi River: Throwing

1. Sit-up throw
2. Forward throw from knees
3. Standing or stepping throw
4. Scoop
5. Hop to throw
6. Catch and throw

Mt. Fuji: Combinations

1. Single butt kick
2. Hurdle hop
3. Single-leg hop
4. Standing triple jump
5. Box skip
6. Box bound

Columbia River: Tossing

1. Shovel
2. Scoop
3. Vertical swing
4. Chest pass
5. Hops to toss
6. Backward hop to toss

The Matterhorn: Vertical work

1. Rocket/star jump
2. Knee-tuck jump
3. Split/scissors jump
4. Power skip
5. Box jump
6. Depth jump

Missouri River: Rotational

1. Half twist
2. Full twist
3. Bar twist
4. Horizontal twist
5. Twist toss
6. Bag thrust/stroke

Mt. McKinley: Horizontal work

1. Prance
2. Gallop
3. Ankle flip
4. Bounding
5. Extended skip
6. Box bounding

Mt. Olympus: Lateral

1. Lateral bound
2. Side hop
3. Incremental vertical hop
4. Diagonal bound
5. Diagonal hop
6. Lateral hop

Chapter 7

Building Power Long Term

Training is organized instruction. However, to organize the instruction you must consider many factors and direct it within a time framework toward specific goals. The final task we undertake in this book is to look at the stretch-shortening cycle in a broad sense, attempting to see as big a picture as possible. Using terms associated with endurance training, muscular hypertrophy training (bodybuilding), and absolute strength training has often been taboo in plyometrics, simply because they tend to be on the other end of the training spectrum from explosion, impulsion, and reaction. When we refer to explosive power training, many of us, purists perhaps, still defend the true intentions of plyometric (i.e., shock-style) training, in which long, slow overdosages intended to produce size or cardiovascular improvements do not often fit. However, using the stretch-shortening cycle can still be a valuable tool to complement those training areas.

Long-term planning and promotion is essential to mastering training and performance, not to mention a sport itself. Program design—encompassing all facets of plyometric training, the stretch-shortening cycle, and evaluation—presents many questions, some answered easily, some with research, and others only with the continual practice of trial, error, retrial, and the passage of documented time.

At some point, progressions (and progress!) take us from development to refinement. Refining power is not ceasing the development process. Rather it is an elite approach to the transitional phase of skill mastery, the extreme specificity of power as it optimally and efficiently applies to the movement, individual, activity, and sport.

We must determine how much stretch-shortening cycle training is needed and where, to achieve sport-specific goals. Once determined, we then analyze performance in the specific training the athlete receives, to continue its use at the same dosages, increased volumes, tapered dosages, or cease the training for specific competitive reasons.

Skillathons—A Way to Evaluate

The skillathons are one method to determine how much or where you need particular training. From research and common practice, these tests have been selected because they assess elastic-reactive improvement in a valid and reliable manner, and they can show areas that lack speed, strength, or agility and coordination, thus allowing us to emphasize work on those weaknesses.

Standing-Landing Jump Tests

There are several methods to evaluate power involving jumping movements. The 12 we mention here are commonly used, and you can assess their standardized measurements.

Vertical Jump

The athlete stands flat-footed next to a wall, pole, or measurement device. Using the tips of the fingers, he or she reaches up and marks the highest point possible.

Remaining in the same place, the athlete will summon all the forces possible by executing a short, quick countermovement jump using flexion of the hips, knees, and ankles, then rapid extension of the entire body and reach arm. At the apex of the jump, the athlete uses the tips of the fingers to record the highest mark possible. The distance between the standing-reach mark and the jumping-reach mark is the recorded score. Take the best of three to five trials. Emphasize executing the jumps without moving the feet before takeoff in a shuffling or stepping action. Often coaches will allow a step or even a several-step approach. You may want to consider this for evaluating specific jump parameters (e.g., approach jumps in volleyball or speed versus power jumping evaluations), as long as you maintain the validity of the vertical jump test. The test determines height of rise of center of gravity. Continually charting these results can offer insight about what form of training, as in speed and elastic-reactive versus core or relative strength, may be lacking in a person's dynamic development.

Depth Jump

Using boxes of different heights or a stair-step apparatus, the athlete drops from levels between 12 and 42 inches onto grass or a firm but resilient mat. Upon landing, the athlete immediately jumps upward to reach or surpass the mark placed on the wall during the vertical jump test. The athlete continues to move to a higher drop until he or she can no longer attain the same jump height as in the vertical jump. Allow one or two minutes of rest between each trial for the muscle systems to recover.

The point of the depth or drop height when the athlete attained maximum vertical jump (rebound) height is the approximate height to train for in this type of plyometric exercise. Studies have recommended that drop heights should not exceed 16 to 24 inches. Our studies show that a further reduction in drop height may be appropriate (8 to 24 inches) as indicated in chapter 3.

Jumps Decathlon

The following series of takeoff, flight, and landing drills and the evaluation measurements are competitive combinations of jumps arranged to provide work, fun, and a means for testing the athlete's progressive capabilities. Wilf Paish compiled these jumping decathlon tables, and we give them here as D.C.V. Watts represented them in an instructional booklet on long jumping (Watts 1968). The tables were compiled graphically and extended to cover the lower-ability ranges. In most cases, the top mark is that of the approximate world record for the event set by professional jumpers of the late eighteen hundreds (see table 7.1). The mean for the five-stride long jump is from tests once given to specialist jumpers.

Do not use these tables to compare one leaping event with another, but mainly to encourage leaping and bounding as training for other events with a little competitive spirit attached. The events are not listed in any particular order.

Make the standing long jump with both feet together, using the arms to aid in lift. Measure to the nearest point of contact. The standing triple jump is with the takeoff foot in flat contact with the ground and the noncontact leg able to swing freely. This rule applies to the other hop and step combinations. The two hops, step, and jump; two hops, two steps, and jump; and two hops, two steps, and two jumps use a two-foot takeoff on the second of the two jumps. The five spring jumps is five consecutive double-leg bounds. Keep the feet together and the movement continuous. The standing four hops and jump starts like the standing triple jump. In the running four hops and jump the length of the run is unlimited. The 25-yard hop begins from a standing position. In most hopping measurements the tables are compiled for the dominant leg, although you should test both legs and record a possible mean for right and left. The five-stride long jump employs regular jumping rules, except the run is limited to five strides. Allow two or three successful attempts per each event. This is a good single training session for any athlete seeking to train intensely for power (Paish 1968).

Table 7.1   Jumping Decathlon Tables

	1	2	3	4	5	6	7	8	9	10
	Standing long jump	Standing triple jump	2 hops, step, and jump	2 hops, 2 steps, and jump	2 hops, 2 steps, 2 jumps	5 spring jumps	Standing 4 hops and jump	Running 4 hops and jump	25-yd. hop (dominant leg)	5-stride long jump
100	12' 3"	34' 6"	42' 8"	51' 0"	62' 10"	56' 0"	58' 0"	78' 0"	2.5 s	23' 11"
99	-	34' 3"	42' 4"	50' 9"	62' 4"	55' 6"	57' 6"	77' 6"	-	-
98	12' 0"	34' 0"	42' 0"	50' 6"	61' 10"	55' 0"	57' 0"	77' 0"	2.6	-
97	-	33' 9"	41' 8"	50' 3"	61' 4"	54' 6"	56' 6"	76' 6"	-	23' 10"
96	11' 9"	33' 6"	41' 4"	49' 6"	60' 10"	54' 0"	56' 0"	76' 0"	2.7	-
95	-	33' 3"	41' 0"	49' 3"	60' 4"	53' 10"	55' 8"	75' 6"	-	-
94	11' 6"	33' 0"	40' 8"	48' 10"	59' 10"	53' 4"	55' 4"	75' 0"	2.8	23' 9"
93	-	32' 9"	40' 4"	48' 6"	59' 4"	53' 0"	55' 0"	74' 6"	-	-
92	11' 3"	32' 6"	40' 0"	48' 2"	58' 10"	52' 6"	54' 6"	74' 0"	2.9	-
91	-	32' 3"	39' 8"	47' 10"	58' 4"	52' 0"	54' 0"	73' 4"	-	23' 8"
90	11' 0"	32' 0"	39' 4"	47' 6"	57' 10"	51' 10"	53' 8"	72' 2"	3.0 s	-
89	-	31' 9"	39' 0"	47' 2"	57' 4"	51' 4"	53' 4"	71' 6"	-	-
88	10' 9"	31' 6"	38' 8"	46' 10"	56' 10"	51' 0"	53' 0"	71' 0"	3.1	23' 7"
87	-	31' 3"	38' 4"	46' 6"	56' 4"	50' 6"	52' 6"	70' 6"	-	-
86	10' 6"	31' 0"	38' 0"	46' 0"	55' 10"	50' 0"	52' 0"	70' 0"	3.2	-
85	-	30' 9"	37' 8"	45' 10"	55' 6"	49' 10"	51' 8"	69' 6"	-	23' 6"
84	10' 3"	30' 6"	37' 4"	45' 6"	55' 0"	49' 4"	51' 4"	69' 0"	3.3	-
83	-	30' 3"	37' 0"	45' 2"	54' 8"	49' 0"	51' 0"	68' 3"	3.4	23' 5"
82	10' 0"	30' 0"	36' 8"	44' 10"	54' 2"	48' 8"	50' 8"	67' 9"	3.5	-
81	-	29' 9"	36' 4"	44' 6"	53' 8"	48' 2"	50' 4"	67' 0"	3.6	23' 4"
80	9' 9"	29' 6"	36' 0"	44' 2"	53' 2"	47' 10"	50' 0"	66' 6"	3.7	-
79	-	29' 3"	35' 8"	43' 10"	52' 10"	47' 4"	49' 6"	66' 0"	3.8	23' 3"
78	9' 6"	29' 0"	35' 4"	43' 6"	52' 6"	47' 0"	49' 0"	65' 6"	3.9	-
77	-	28' 9"	35' 0"	43' 0"	52' 0"	46' 8"	48' 8"	65' 0"	4.0 s	23' 2"
76	9' 3"	28' 6"	34' 8"	42' 10"	51' 6"	46' 2"	48' 4"	64' 3"	4.1	23' 1"
75	-	28' 3"	34' 4"	42' 6"	51' 0"	45' 10"	48' 0"	63' 9"	4.2	23' 0"
74	9' 0"	28' 0"	34' 0"	42' 2"	50' 6"	45' 6"	47' 6"	63' 0"	4.3	22' 10"
73	8' 10"	27' 9"	33' 8"	41' 10"	50' 0"	45' 0"	47' 0"	62' 6"	4.4	22' 8"
72	8' 9"	27' 6"	33' 4"	41' 6"	49' 8"	44' 8"	46' 8"	62' 0"	4.5	22' 6"
71	8' 8"	27' 3"	33' 0"	41' 0"	49' 4"	44' 4"	46' 4"	61' 6"	4.6	22' 4"
70	8' 7"	27' 0"	32' 8"	40' 9"	48' 10"	44' 0"	46' 0"	61' 0"	4.7	22' 2"
69	8' 6"	26' 9"	32' 4"	40' 6"	48' 4"	43' 6"	45' 6"	60' 6"	4.8	22' 0"
68	8' 5"	26' 6"	32' 0"	40' 0"	48' 0"	43' 0"	45' 0"	60' 0"	4.9	21' 9"
67	8' 4"	26' 3"	31' 8"	39' 8"	47' 6"	42' 8"	44' 8"	59' 6"	5.0 s	21' 6"
66	8' 3"	26' 0"	31' 4"	39' 4"	47' 0"	42' 4"	44' 4"	59' 0"	5.1	21' 3"
65	8' 2"	25' 9"	31' 0"	39' 0"	46' 8"	42' 0"	44' 0"	58' 3"	5.2	21' 0"
64	8' 1"	25' 6"	30' 8"	38' 8"	46' 2"	41' 8"	43' 8"	57' 9"	5.3	20' 9"
63	8' 0"	25' 3"	30' 4"	38' 4"	45' 10"	41' 4"	43' 4"	57' 0"	5.4	20' 6"
62	7' 11"	25' 0"	30' 0"	38' 0"	45' 4"	41' 0"	43' 0"	56' 6"	5.5	20' 3"
61	7' 10"	24' 9"	29' 8"	37' 8"	45' 0"	40' 6"	42' 6"	56' 0"	5.6	20' 0"
60	7' 9"	24' 6"	29' 4"	37' 4"	44' 6"	40' 0"	42' 0"	55' 6"	5.7	19' 9"
59	7' 8"	24' 3"	29' 0"	37' 0"	44' 0"	39' 6"	41' 6"	55' 0"	5.8	19' 6"
58	7' 7"	24' 0"	28' 8"	36' 8"	43' 6"	39' 0"	41' 0"	54' 3"	5.9	19' 3"
57	7' 6"	23' 9"	28' 4"	36' 4"	43' 0"	38' 8"	40' 8"	53' 9"	6.0 s	19' 0"
56	7' 5"	23' 6"	28' 0"	36' 0"	42' 6"	38' 4"	40' 4"	53' 0"	6.1	18' 9"
55	7' 4"	23' 3"	27' 9"	35' 8"	42' 0"	38' 0"	40' 0"	52' 6"	6.2	18' 6"
54	7' 3"	23' 0"	27' 6"	35' 4"	41' 6"	37' 8"	39' 8"	52' 0"	6.3	18' 3"
53	7' 2"	22' 9"	27' 3"	35' 0"	41' 0"	37' 4"	39' 4"	51' 6"	6.4	18' 0"
52	7' 1"	22' 6"	27' 0"	34' 8"	40' 6"	37' 0"	38' 0"	51' 0"	6.5	17' 9"
51	7' 0"	22' 3"	26' 9"	34' 4"	40' 0"	36' 8"	37' 6"	50' 6"	6.6	17' 6"

	1	2	3	4	5	6	7	8	9	10
	Standing long jump	Standing triple jump	2 hops, step, and jump	2 hops, 2 steps, and jump	2 hops, 2 steps, 2 jumps	5 spring jumps	Standing 4 hops and jump	Running 4 hops and jump	25-yd. hop (dominant leg)	5-stride long jump
50	6' 11"	22' 0"	26' 6"	34' 0"	39' 6"	36' 4"	37' 0"	50' 0"	6.7	17' 3"
49	6' 10"	21' 9"	26' 3"	33' 8"	39' 0"	36' 0"	36' 8"	49' 6"	6.8	17' 0"
48	6' 9"	21' 6"	26' 0"	33' 4"	38' 6"	35' 8"	36' 4"	49' 0"	-	16' 10"
47	6' 8"	21' 3"	25' 9"	33' 0"	38' 0"	35' 4"	36' 0"	48' 6"	6.9	16' 8"
46	6' 7"	21' 0"	25' 6"	32' 8"	37' 6"	35' 0"	35' 6"	48' 0"	-	16' 6"
45	6' 6"	20' 9"	25' 3"	32' 4"	37' 0"	34' 8"	35' 0"	47' 6"	7.0 s	16' 4"
44	6' 5"	20' 6"	25' 0"	32' 0"	36' 8"	34' 4"	34' 6"	47' 0"	-	16' 2"
43	6' 4"	20' 3"	24' 9"	31' 8"	36' 4"	34' 0"	34' 0"	46' 6"	7.1	16' 0"
42	6' 3"	20' 0"	24' 6"	31' 4"	36' 0"	33' 8"	33' 6"	46' 0"	-	15' 10"
41	6' 2"	19' 9"	24' 3"	31' 0"	35' 8"	33' 4"	33' 0"	45' 6"	7.2	15' 8"
40	6' 1"	19' 6"	24' 0"	30' 8"	35' 4"	33' 0"	32' 6"	45' 0"	-	15' 6"
39	6' 0"	19' 3"	23' 9"	30' 4"	35' 0"	32' 8"	32' 0"	44' 6"	7.3	15' 4"
38	5' 11"	19' 0"	23' 6"	30' 0"	34' 8"	32' 4"	31' 6"	44' 0"	-	15' 2"
37	5' 10"	18' 9"	23' 3"	29' 8"	34' 4"	32' 0"	31' 0"	43' 6"	7.4	15' 0"
36	5' 9"	18' 6"	23' 0"	29' 4"	34' 0"	31' 8"	30' 8"	43' 0"	-	14' 10"
35	5' 8"	18' 3"	22' 9"	29' 0"	33' 8"	31' 4"	30' 4"	42' 6"	7.5	14' 8"
34	5' 7"	18' 0"	22' 6"	28' 8"	33' 4"	31' 0"	30' 0"	42' 0"	-	14' 6"
33	5' 6"	17' 9"	22' 3"	28' 4"	33' 0"	30' 8"	29' 8"	41' 6"	7.6	14' 4"
32	5' 5"	17' 6"	22' 0"	28' 0"	32' 8"	30' 4"	29' 4"	41' 0"	-	14' 2"
31	5' 4"	17' 3"	21' 9"	27' 8"	32' 4"	30' 0"	29' 0"	40' 6"	7.7	14' 0"
30	5' 3"	17' 0"	21' 6"	27' 4"	32' 0"	29' 8"	28' 8"	40' 0"	-	13' 10"
29	5' 2"	16' 9"	21' 3"	27' 0"	31' 8"	29' 4"	28' 4"	39' 6"	7.8	13' 8"
28	5' 1"	16' 6"	21' 0"	26' 8"	31' 4"	29' 0"	28' 0"	39' 0"	-	13' 6"
27	5' 0"	16' 3"	20' 9"	26' 4"	31' 0"	28' 8"	27' 8"	38' 6"	7.9	13' 4"
26	4' 11"	16' 0"	20' 6"	26' 0"	30' 8"	28' 4"	27' 4"	38' 0"	-	13' 2"
25	4' 10"	15' 9"	20' 3"	25' 8"	30' 4"	28' 0"	27' 0"	37' 6"	8.0 s	13' 0"
24	4' 9"	15' 6"	20' 0"	25' 4"	30' 0"	27' 8"	26' 8"	37' 0"	-	12' 10"
23	4' 8"	15' 3"	19' 8"	25' 0"	29' 8"	27' 4"	26' 4"	36' 6"	-	12' 8"
22	4' 7"	15' 0"	19' 4"	24' 8"	29' 4"	27' 0"	26' 0"	36' 0"	8.1	12' 6"
21	4' 6"	14' 9"	19' 0"	24' 4"	29' 0"	26' 8"	25' 8"	35' 6"	-	12' 4"
20	4' 5"	14' 6"	18' 8"	24' 0"	28' 8"	26' 4"	25' 4"	35' 0"	-	12' 2"
19	4' 3"	14' 0"	18' 4"	23' 8"	28' 4"	26' 0"	25' 0"	34' 6"	8.2	12' 0"
18	4' 2"	13' 9"	18' 0"	23' 4"	28' 0"	25' 8"	24' 8"	34' 0"	-	11' 10"
17	4' 1"	13' 6"	17' 8"	23' 0"	27' 8"	25' 4"	24' 4"	33' 6"	-	11' 8"
16	4' 0"	13' 3"	17' 4"	22' 8"	27' 4"	25' 0"	24' 0"	33' 0"	8.3	11' 6"
15	3' 11"	13' 0"	17' 0"	22' 4"	27' 0"	24' 8"	23' 8"	32' 6"	-	11' 4"
14	3' 10"	12' 9"	16' 8"	22' 0"	26' 8"	24' 4"	23' 4"	32' 0"	-	11' 2"
13	3' 9"	12' 6"	16' 4"	21' 8"	26' 4"	24' 0"	23' 0"	31' 6"	8.4	11' 0"
12	3' 8"	12' 3"	16' 0"	21' 4"	26' 0"	23' 8"	22' 8"	31' 0"	-	10' 8"
11	3' 7"	12' 0"	15' 8"	21' 0"	25' 8"	23' 4"	22' 4"	30' 6"	-	10' 4"
10	3' 6"	11' 9"	15' 4"	20' 8"	25' 4"	23' 0"	22' 0"	30' 0"	8.5	10' 0"
9	3' 5"	11' 6"	15' 0"	20' 4"	25' 0"	22' 8"	21' 8"	29' 6"	-	9' 8"
8	3' 4"	11' 3"	14' 8"	20' 0"	24' 8"	22' 4"	21' 4"	29' 0"	-	9' 4"
7	3' 3"	11' 0"	14' 4"	19' 8"	24' 4"	22' 0"	21' 0"	28' 6"	8.6	9' 0"
6	3' 2"	10' 9"	14' 0"	19' 4"	24' 0"	21' 8"	20' 8"	28' 0"	-	8' 8"
5	3' 1"	10' 6"	13' 8"	19' 0"	23' 8"	21' 4"	20' 4"	27' 6"	-	8' 4"
4	3' 0"	10' 3"	13' 4"	18' 8"	23' 4"	21' 0"	20' 0"	27' 0"	8.7	8' 0"
3	2' 11"	10' 0"	13' 0"	18' 4"	23' 0"	20' 8"	19' 8"	26' 6"	-	7' 8"
2	2' 10"	9' 9"	12' 8"	18' 0"	22' 8"	20' 4"	19' 4"	26' 0"	-	7' 4"
1	2' 0"	9' 6"	12' 4"	17' 8"	22' 0"	20' 0"	19' 0"	25' 6"	8.8	7' 0"

Throwing and Passing Tests

These tests, most often using a medicine ball or shot, assess upper-body impulsive or explosive capabilities and determine the weight and size of the implements necessary for optimal training.

Medicine Ball Chest Pass

The athlete sits in a straight-back chair, strapped in securely with a belt or waist harness. With a medicine ball of 7, 9, or 11 pounds (4, 5, or 6 kilograms), the athlete performs a chest pass, applying all the forces possible to the put. The distance from the chair to the ball's landing point determines how heavy a ball to use for such exercises. Any passes shorter than approximately 30 feet indicate a need for training with a lighter medicine ball.

Medicine Ball Overhead Throw Forward

The athlete takes a squared stance with the toes of both feet on a line, holding the ball over the head and slightly behind it. The movement begins by flexing the knees out over the toes and arching farther backward with the ball. The body then extends forward, whipping hips, shoulders, elbows, and wrists with such force that the feet come off the ground as the ball propels forward. You can measure the distance in either feet or yards, and adjust the norms to measure accordingly.

Medicine Ball Overhead Throw Backward

The athlete takes a squared stance with the toes of both feet on a line, holding the ball below the hips with the arms long. The movement begins by flexing the knees out over the toes and arching the shoulders farther forward, lowering the ball to the knees. The body then extends backward, whipping hips, shoulders, elbows, and wrists with such force that the feet come off the ground as both the ball and the body propel backward. You can measure the distance in either feet or yards, and adjust the norms to measure accordingly.

Seasonal Conditioning— The Power Hierarchy

We need to make several points on using stretch-shortening cycle training, whether the design is for plyometrics, Olympic lifting, speed work, or agility and mobility. We consider all these types of training as stretch-shortening cycle and see it, as we mentioned in the goals and objectives section, as an all-encompassing entity. The power hierarchy (see figure 7.1) is useful in placing and structuring the types and magnitudes of stretch-shortening cycle work within the scope of a program. As you move through the training phases, you can also move through the training methods within the structure of the power hierarchy.

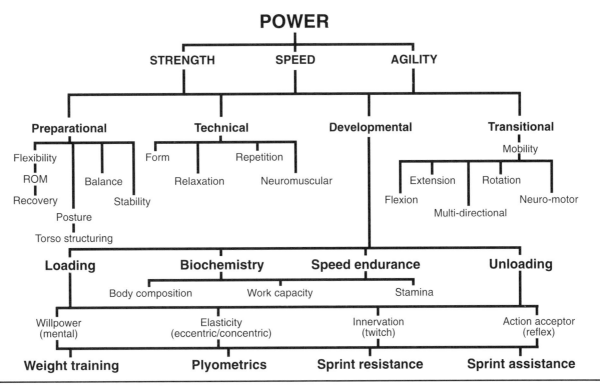

Figure 7.1 The power hierarchy.

Each workout you perform, whether in a weight room, on a court, or on a field, can adhere to the methodologies. You can apply the methodologies to a preparatory session (dynamic and static flexibility), a technical session (form running and lifting movements), a developmental session (all forms of loading, extended durations, and speeds), and a transitional mobility session (changes of direction, high-speed executions).

As you can see in the hierarchy and the workout samples within it, you can accomplish a great deal of stretch-shortening cycle work throughout. As you progress through the teaching or learning stages of the program, each level has a definite place in the hierarchy's workout plan. For example, the teaching progression of pogo, prancing, galloping, and so on, which was the main focus of the plyometric and loading workout for beginning the program, can eventually become part of the technical period (form running) and even the preparatory period (dynamic warm-up). This allows constant attention to developing biomechanical skills in their parts while you progress to the more complex and intense forms of stretch-shortening cycle training as a whole. Often the planner wonders when to emphasize plyometric drills versus weight training and vice versa. When working within the context of the hierarchy and the progressions we provide, the main concern is the goals and objectives for that given cycle in the training phase.

If the weight training includes postural and dynamic forms of lifting (which we think it should), when you apply the specific training method merely depends on the placement of the workout session. Some trainers and sport scientists suggest including training sessions that involve warm-up, dynamic work, followed by strength work, followed by speed work, then cool-down. This is one form of planning, as is the hierarchy method, for establishing when to emphasize the degree of workload.

Year-Round Conditioning— Planned Performance Training

When planning your training, or an athlete's, and the goals and objectives of the program, begin with the peaks or final competitions and work backward from this point. Whether it is a single competitive situation (Tour de France), a portion of a season (state playoffs), or a multipeaking schedule (national, Pan-American, world, or Olympic championships), you can plan for each goal by using the evaluation continuums and the program hierarchy to map the route of the stretch-shortening cycle training in each period of the year's plan (see figure 7.2).

Figure 7.2 The yearly overview.

The Year in Periodized Planning

Just as there is progressing and cycling through a teaching and training format for stretch-shortening cycle or plyometric methodology, you can progress and cycle through the phases, periods, and years—both short term and long term. You can plan periods for the individuals and teams. If you decide on the principle of multilateral periodization (i.e., involving several systems of training) and progress from general to specific, you should expose younger athletes to mixed or multidirectional training as mentioned with the previous hierarchy concepts. It is possible to expose the advanced athletes, those who've developed high levels of core, relative, and dynamic strength, to prioritized or unidirectional (i.e., highly specific) training. In some conditions, you may perform no conventional strength training in a microcycle dominated by elastic-reactive training. In all cases, the repetitions, sets, and rest periods should reflect the training objective.

The Periods

Each period of the training year takes on a different meaning in the array of programs to optimize training. For some, it is merely a change of seasons, in-season and competitive, postseason and regenerative, off-season and general preparatory, and preseason and special preparatory. For others, those dealing with multisport athletes or logistics that allow only in-season training, these periods take on different interpretations. In many situations, the competitive period is a time to back off ardent stretch-shortening cycle and plyometric training other than those specific skills and drills that make up the competition objectives (specific jumping, sprinting, and changing of direction). Developing power can now take a back seat to refining specific speed skills. However, for the period of in-season attention only (e.g., the multisport athlete), an individual may miss all opportunities for basic and special development. Applying methodologies within the power hierarchy can be helpful in both cases. The stretch-shortening cycle (SSC) is evident in many forms of preparatory, or technical work, as well as developmental loading and specific transitional work (see figure 7.3a for those new to plyometrics and 7.3b for those experienced in explosive power). The program planner can prioritize the training cycles within the competitive period, formulating a miniature version of the combination of periods.

In summary, the periods are steps toward the height of performance. Here's an outline:

- Postseason is the transitional period with the objectives of
  1. recovering, restoring, and regenerating from the previous competitive season;
  2. developing or rehabilitating work capacity in strength, acceleration, and mobility; and
  3. making technical readjustments and refinements.

- Off-season is the preparatory period with the objectives of
  1. progressively developing work capacities in strength, speed, and agility; and
  2. technically advancing and evaluating performance in competitive situations.

- Preseason is the precompetitive period with the objectives of
  1. refining specific work capacities in strength, speed, and agility with conversions to specific power and speed endurance;
  2. specifically advancing performance in the competitive situation;
  3. tapering the training model; and
  4. heightening the performance methodologies.

- In-season is the competitive period with the objectives of
  1. expanding the competition experience;
  2. maintaining development of the power and specific speed and speed-endurance skills;
  3. advancing specific techniques;
  4. preparing for competition climax; and
  5. achieving an optimally high performance at the finish of the competition period.

a

Preparation		Evaluation	
Transition	Preparatory	Pre-competitive	Competitive
Regeneration	Technical enhancement	Developmental refinement	Specific maintenance
Program basics 1st 12 weeks	Program basics Repeat 12 week	Desireable dozens 12 week segment	Tapered basics Technical and preparational
0-2 years training ages from beginner to intermediate			

Qualitative   **Quantitative**

➡️

How well   **How much**

b

Preparation		Evaluation	
Transition	Preparatory	Pre-competitive	Competitive
Regeneration	Technical enhancement	Developmental refinement	Specific maintenance
Program basics Continuum work Simple progressions	Desireable dozens Continuum work More specific progressions	Specific development Work cycles Mountains & rivers	Tapered preparational and technical work Continuum revisited
2 + years of training age intermediate to advanced stages			

Figure 7.3 (a) Use of SSC in early training periodization; (b) use of SSC in advanced periodization.

The Phases

As Tudor Bompa (1983) has suggested, each period has certain cycled phases that generate the advancement to specific objectives for each training season. It is not uncommon to see recommendations for plyometric training that continue over several months. Indeed, we believe you can adhere to a continuous, year-round approach. There is a belief that you should use plyometric drills for only three or four weeks of training microcycles. This may come from some practitioner's notion of a limited ability to train certain speed segments. Sergio Zanon (1989), for example, recommends a "cyclic oscillatory trend" of increased plyometric use for 10 days, then decreased for 10 days, regulated over a 3-week cycle. When using a progressive system of stress-continuum plyometrics, we believe that you can use elastic-reactive movements throughout the training phase, at least until major competitive peaking cycles occur. Because of the proprioceptive progress that you can make, this can offer the advantage of year-round stretch-shortening and plyometric attention.

At the end of the chapter we offer samples of possible procedures through a period of training phases. Observe that you can rotate the charts of the annual plans to fit numerous activities and their goals and objectives. You should apply the principles we've discussed of the progressive patterns through the stretch-shortening cycle and plyometric forms of training. Consider their suitability in the hierarchy of power development. Then you can emphasize different areas of stretch-shortening cycle development, be it a dynamic warm-up; technical, developmental, or specific mobility work within the training workouts; or competitive practices in each phase.

Table 7.2		Projected dosage guidelines				
Week number		Load Intensity	Daily average (volumes) number exercises, sets, and reps			Sprint development
			Weights	Plyometrics	Agilities	
1	Stages	Low	[3 day] [4 day] 241 / 194	3-4×2×4-8 (42)	1×2-3×2 (4)	Accl./Tech./ARCp. 2-4×4-8×50
2		Low/ Medium	324 / 256	3-4×2-3×4-8 (53)	2×2-3×2 (8)	Accl./Load/ARCp. 2-4×4-8×60
3	General adaptation	Medium	349 / 271	3-4×2-3×4-10 (61)	2-3×3×2 (12)	Accl./Load/ANRCp. 2-4×4-8×70
4	General core strength	Low/ Medium	289 / 235	4×2-3×6-10 (80)	3×3×2 (18)	Accl./Load/ANRCp. 2-4×6-10×60-80
5		Medium	200 / 161	4-5×2-3×6-10 (90)	3-4×3×4 (42)	Accl./Load/Overspeed 2-4×6-10×60-90
6	Maximum strength	Medium/ High	151 / 117	4-5×2-3×6-12 (101)	4×3×4 (48)	Accl./Contrast 2×6-12×40-100
7		Medium	123 / 99	5×2-3×6-12 (112)	3×4×4 (48)	Accl./Contrast 2-4×6-10×40-100
8	Maximum strength and power	Medium/ High	117 / 94	5×2-3×8-12 (125)	3×4×4 (48)	Accl./Contrast 2-4×6-10×40-90
9		High	106 / 86	4×2-3×10-12 (110)	2×4×4 (32)	Speed/Contrast 2-4×4-8×40-90
10	Complexes and combinations	Medium/ High	74 / 56	3-4×2×10-12 (77)	2×3×4 (24)	Speed/Contrast 2-4×4-8×20-60
11	Transition	High	54 / 54	2×2×10-12 (44)	2×2×4 (16)	Speed 2-4×2-4×20-40
12		Evaluation / break				

References and
Suggested Readings

Adams, T.M. 1984. An investigation of selected plyometric training exercises on muscular leg strength and power. *Track and Field Quarterly Review* 84 (4): 36-39.

Albert, Mark. 1991. *Eccentric muscle training in sports and orthopaedics.* New York: Churchill Livingstone.

Aoki, H., R. Tsukahara, and K. Yabe. 1989. Effects of pre-motion electromyographic silent period on dynamic force exertion during a rapid ballistic movement in man. *European Journal of Applied Physiology* 58 (4): 426-432.

Asmussen, E., and F. Bonde-Petersen. 1974a. Storage of elastic energy in skeletal muscles in man. *Acta Physiologica Scandinavia* 91: 385-392.

Asmussen, E., and F. Bonde-Petersen. 1974b. Apparent efficiency and storage of elastic energy in human muscles during exercise. *Acta Physiologica Scandinavia* 92: 537-545.

Aura, O., and J.T. Viitasalo. 1989. Biomechanical characteristics of jumping. *International Journal of Sport Biomechanics* 5: 89-98.

Blattner, S.E., and L. Noble. 1979. Relative effects of isokinetic and plyometric training on vertical jump performance. *Research Quarterly* 50: 583-588.

Bobbert, M.F., M. Mackey, D. Schinkelshoek, P. Huijing, and G. van Ingen Schenau. 1986. Biomechanical analysis of drop and countermovement jumps. *European Journal of Applied Physiology* 54: 566-573.

Bobbert, M.F., P.A. Huijing, and G.J. van Ingen Schenau. 1987a. Drop jumping I: The influence of jumping technique on the biomechanics of jumping. *Medicine and Science in Sports and Exercise* 19: 332-338.

Bobbert, M.F., P.A. Huijing, and G.J. van Ingen Schenau. 1987b. Drop jumping II: The influence of drop heights on the biomechanics of drop jumping. *Medicine and Science in Sports and Exercise* 19: 339-346.

Bompa, T. 1983. *Theory and methodology of training, the key to athletic performance*. Dubuque, IA: Kendall/Hunt.

Bompa, T. 1993. *Periodization of strength, the new wave in strength training*. Toronto: Veritas.

Bosco, C. 1982. Physiological considerations of strength and explosive power and jumping drills (plyometric exercise). Conference proceedings on planning for elite performance (pp. 27-37). Ottawa, ON: Canadian Track and Field Association.

Bosco, C. 1985. Force-velocity relationship and sport performance. *Sports Biomechanics Newsletter* 2: 4-5.

Bosco, C., and P.V. Komi. 1979. Mechanical characteristics and fiber composition of human leg extensor muscles. *European Journal of Applied Physiology* 41: 275-284.

Bosco C., and P.V. Komi. 1981. Potentiation of the mechanical behavior of the human skeletal muscle through prestretching. *Acta Physiologica Scandinavia* 106: 467-472.

Bosco, C., and P.V. Komi. 1982. Muscle elasticity in athletes. In *Exercise and sport biology* (pp. 109-117), edited by P.V. Komi. Champaign, IL: International Series on Sports Sciences.

Bosco C., P.V. Komi, and A. Ito. 1981. Prestretch potentiation of human skeletal muscle during the ballistic movement. *Acta Physiology Scandinavia* 111 (2): 273-282.

Cavagna, G.A. 1977. Storage and utilization of elastic energy in skeletal muscle. *Exercise and Sports Science Review* 5: 89-129.

Cavagna, G.A., B. Dusman, and R. Margaria. 1968. Positive work done by a previously stretched muscle. *Journal of Applied Physiology* 24: 21-32.

Cavagna, G.A., F. Saibene, and R. Margaria. 1964. Mechanical work in running. *Journal of Applied Physiology* 19: 249-256.

Cavagna, G.A., F. Saibene, and R. Margaria. 1965. Effect of negative work on the amount of positive work performed by an isolated muscle. *Journal of Applied Physiology* 20:157-158.

Cavagna, G.A., L. Komarek, G. Citterio, and R. Margaria. 1971. Power output of a previously stretched muscle. In *Medicine and sport, biomechanics II* (pp.159-167), edited by J. Vredenbregt and J. Wartenweiler. Basel: Karger.

Chapman, A.E. 1985. The mechanical properties of human muscle. *Exercise and Sport Science Review* 13: 443-501.

Clutch, D., M. Wilton, C. McGowan, and G.R. Bryce. 1983. The effects of depth jumps and weight training on leg strength and vertical jump. *Research Quarterly for Exercise and Sport* 54:5-10.

Costello, F. 1984. Using weight training and plyometrics to increase explosive power for football. *National Strength and Conditioning Association Journal* 6 (2): 22-25.

Curwin, S., and W.D. Stanish. 1984. *Tendinitis: Its etiology and treatment*. Lexington, MA: Collamore Press.

Dick, F. 1984. *Training theory*. London: British Amateur Athletic Board.

Dietz, V., D. Schmidtbleicher, and J. Noth. 1979. Neuronal mechanisms of human locomotion. *Journal of Neurophysiology* 42: 1212-1222.

Ebbeling, C.B., and P.M. Clarkson. 1990. Muscle adaptation prior to recovery following eccentric exercise. *European Journal of Applied Physiology* 60 (1): 26-31.

Fox, E.L. 1979. *Sports physiology*. Philadelphia: Saunders.

Fox, E.L., and D. Mathews. 1981. *The physiological basis of physical education and athletics*. Philadelphia: Saunders.

Frid'en, J. 1984. Changes in human skeletal muscle induced by long term eccentric exercise. *Cell Tissue Research* 236 (2): 365-372.

Frid'en, J., P.N. Sfakianos, and A.R. Hargens. 1986. Muscle soreness and intra muscular fluid pressure: Comparison between eccentric and concentric load. *Journal of Applied Physiology* 61 (6): 2175-2179.

Fritz V.K., and W.T. Stauber. 1988. Characterization of muscles injured by forced lengthening II. Proteoglycans. *Medicine and Science in Sports and Exercise* 20 (4): 354-361.

Gambetta, V. 1977. Plyometric training. *Athletica* 4 (5): 15-17.

Gambetta, V. 1981. Plyometric training. In *Track and field coaching manual* (pp. 58-59), edited by V. Gambetta. West Point, NY: Leisure Press.

Gambetta, V. 1985. Plyometric training. In *The Athletics Congress track and field coaching manual* (pp. 34-36), edited by V. Gambetta. Champaign, IL: Human Kinetics.

Gambetta, V. 1986. Velocity of shortening as an explanation for the training effect of plyometric training. The second Allerton Symposium, G. Winkler (Chair), Track and Field Training, November, at Monticello, IL.

Gambetta, V. 1989. Plyometrics for beginners—Basic considerations. *New Studies in Athletics, IAAF Quarterly* 4: 61-64.

Gambetta, V., R. Rogers, R. Fields, D. Semenick, and J. Radcliffe. 1986. NSCA plyometric videotape symposium, Lincoln, NE.

Gowitzke, B.A., and M. Milner. 1988. Scientific basis of human movement. 3d ed. Baltimore: Williams & Wilkins.

Guyton, A.C. 1981. *Textbook of medical physiology*. Philadelphia: Saunders.

Hakkinen, K., M. Alen, and P.V. Komi. 1985. Changes in isometric force- and relaxation-time, electromyographic and muscle fiber characteristics of human skeletal muscle during strength training and detraining. *Acta Physiologica Scandinavia* 125: 573-585.

Harre, D. 1982. *Principles of sports training—Introduction to the theory and methods of training*. Berlin: Sportverlag.

Hill, A.V. 1938. The heat of shortening and the dynamic constants of muscle. *Proceedings of the Royal Society of London* (Biology) 126: 136-195.

Hill, A.V. 1950. The series elastic component of muscle (summary). *Proceedings of the Royal Society of London* (Biology) 137: 273-280.

Huxley, H.E. 1969. The mechanism of muscular contraction. *Science* 164: 1356-1366.

Jacoby, E., and B. Fraley. 1995. *Complete book of jumps*. Champaign, IL: Human Kinetics.

Kachaev, S.V. 1984. Methods of developing speed-strength (explosiveness) in young track and field athletes. *The Soviet Sports Review* 19 (1): 44-49.

Katz, B. 1939. The relation between force and speed in muscular contraction. *Journal of Physiology* 96: 45-64.

King, I. 1993. Plyometric training: In perspective. Parts 1 and 2. *Science Periodical on Research and Technology in Sport* 13 (5 and 6).

Kisner, C., and L.A. Colby. 1990. *Therapeutic exercise, foundations and techniques*. 2d ed. Philadelphia: Davis.

Komi, P.V. 1973. Measurement of the force-velocity relationship in human muscle under concentric and eccentric contractions. *Medicine and Sport: Biomechanics III* 8: 224-229.

Komi, P.V. 1984a. Biomechanics and neuromuscular performance. *Medicine and Science in Sport and Exercise* 16: 26-28.

Komi, P.V. 1984b. Physiological and biomechanical correlates of muscle function: Effects of muscle structure and stretch-shortening cycle on force and speed. In *Exercise and Sports Science Reviews* 12: 81-121, edited by R.L. Terjung. Lexington, MA: Collamore Press.

Komi, P.V. 1986. The stretch-shortening cycle and human power output. In *Human muscle power*, edited by N.L. Jones, N. McCartney, and A. McComas. Champaign, IL: Human Kinetics.

Komi, P.V., ed. 1992. *Strength and power in sport*. Oxford: Blackwell Scientific.

Komi, P.V., and C. Bosco. 1978. Utilization of stored elastic energy in leg extensor muscles by men and women. *Medicine and Science in Sports* 10: 261-265.

Lamb, D.R. 1984. Physiology of exercise, responses and adaptations. Rev. ed. New York: Macmillan.

Landis, D. 1983. Big skinny kids. *National Strength and Conditioning Association Journal* 5: 26-29.

Luhtanen, P., and P.V. Komi. 1980. Force, power, and elasticity—velocity relationships in walking, running, and jumping. *European Journal of Applied Physiology* 44: 279-289.

Matveyev, L. 1977. *Fundamentals of sports training.* Moscow: Progress.

McArdle, W., F.I. Katch, and V.L. Katch. 1981. *Exercise physiology, energy, nutrition and human performance.* Philadelphia: Lea & Febiger.

McFarlane, B. 1982. Jumping exercises. *Track and Field Quarterly Review* 82 (4): 54-55.

Nardone, A., C. Romano, and M. Schieppati. 1989. Selective recruitment of high-threshold human motor units during voluntary isotonic lengthening of active muscles. *Journal of Physiology London* 409: 451-471.

Newham, D.J., K.R. Mills, B.M. Quigley, and R.H. Edwards. 1983. Pain and fatigue after concentric and eccentric muscle contractions. *Clinical Science* 64 (1): 55-62.

Paish, W. 1968. The jumps decathlon tables. In D.C.V. Watts, *The long jump.* London: Amateur Athletic Association.

Polhemus, R. 1981. Plyometric training for the improvement of athletic ability. *Scholastic Coach* 51 (4): 68-69.

Radcliffe, J., and L. Osternig. 1995. Effects on performance of variable eccentric loads during depth jumps. *Journal of Sport Rehabilitation* 4: 31-41.

Radcliffe, J.C., and R.C. Farentinos. 1985. *Plyometrics explosive power training.* Champaign, IL: Human Kinetics.

Reid, P. 1989. Plyometrics and the high jump. *New Studies in Athletics* 4 (1): 67-74.

Robertson, R.N. 1984. Compliance characteristics of human muscle during dynamic and static loading conditions (abstract). Clinical symposium. *Medicine and Science in Sports and Exercise* 16: 186.

Sale, D. 1991. Testing strength and power. In *Physiological testing of the high performance athlete* (pp. 21-106). Rev. ed., edited by J.D. MacDougall, H.A. Wenger, and H.J. Green. Champaign, IL: Human Kinetics.

Schmidtbleicher, D. 1992. Training for power events. In *Strength and power in sport* (pp. 381-395), edited by P.V. Komi. Oxford: Blackwell Scientific.

Scoles, G. 1978. Depth jumping! Does it really work? *The Athletic Journal* 58 (5) 48-49, 74-75.

Siff, M., and Y. Verkhoshansky. 1996. *SuperTraining, special strength training for sporting excellence.* 2d ed. Pittsburgh: Sports Support Syndicate.

Sinclair, A. 1981. A reaction to depth jumping. *Sports Coach* 5 (2): 24-25.

Stauber, W. 1989. Eccentric action of muscles: Physiology, injury, and adaptation. *Exercise and Sport Science Reviews* 17: 157-185.

Stauber, W., V.K. Fritz, D.W. Vogelbach, and B. Dahlman. 1988. Characterization of muscles injured by forced lengthening I. Cellular infiltrates. *Medicine and Science in Sports and Exercise* 20 (4): 345-353.

Tansley, J. 1980. *The flop book.* Santa Monica, CA: Peterson Lithograph.

Thayer, B. 1981. Plyometrics. *Coaching Review* Sept/Oct (4): 18-19.

Valik, B. 1966. Strength preparation of young track and fielders. *Physical Culture in School* 4: 28. In *Yessis Translation Review* (1967) 2: 56-60.

Vander, J.A., J.H. Sherman, and D.S. Luciano. 1980. *Human physiology* (pp.144-190). Rev. ed. New York: McGraw-Hill.

van Ingen Schenau, G.J., M.F. Bobbert, P.A. Huijing, and R.D. Woittiez. 1985. The instantaneous torque-angular velocity relation in plantar flexion during jumping. *Medicine and Science in Sports and Exercise* 17: 422-426.

Verkhoshansky, Y. 1968. Are depth jumps useful? *Yessis Review of Soviet Physical Education and Sports* 3: 75-78.

Verkhoshansky, Y. 1969. Perspectives in the improvement of speed-strength preparation of jumpers. *Yessis Review of Soviet Physical Education and Sports* 4: 28-34.

Verkhoshansky, Y., and G. Chernousov. 1974. Jumps in the training of a sprinter. *Track and Field* 9: 16. In *Review of Soviet Physical Education and Sports* (1974) 9: 62-66.

Verkhoshansky, Y., and V. Tatyan. 1973. Speed-strength preparation of future champions. *Legkaya Atletica* 2: 12-13.

Viitasalo, J.T. and Bosco, C. 1982. Electromechanical behaviour of human muscles in vertical jumps. *European Journal of Applied Physiology* 48: 253-261.

Vorobyev, A. 1978. *A textbook on weightlifting.* Budapest: International Weightlifting Federation.

Webster, D. 1969. *New world dictionary of the American language.* Rev. ed. New York: World.

Wilson, G.J., R.U. Newton, A.J. Murphy, and B.J. Humphries. 1993. The optimal training load for the development of dynamic athletic performance. *Medicine and Science in Sports and Exercise* 25 (11): 1279-1286.

Wilt, F. 1975. Plyometrics, what it is—how it works. *Athletic Journal* 9 (76): 89-90.

Wilt, F., and T. Ecker. 1970. *International track and field coaching encyclopedia.* West Nyack, NY: Parker.

Winter, D.A. 1979. *Biomechanics of human movement.* New York: Wiley.

Young, W. 1993. Training for speed/strength: Heavy vs. light loads. *National Strength and Conditioning Association Journal* 15 (5): 34-42.

Zanon, S. 1974. Plieometry in jumping. *Die Lehre der Leichtathletik* 16: 1-13.

Zanon, S. 1989. Plyometrics: Past and present. *New Studies in Athletics* 4 (1): 7-17.

About the Authors

When you want reliable training techniques, you want the best information from the most qualified sources. In addition to coauthoring *Plyometrics, Explosive Power Training* in 1985, **James Radcliffe** and **Robert Farentinos** have worked for years with countless elite athletes who have reaped huge benefits from high-powered plyometric training.

Jim Radcliffe is the head strength and conditioning coach at the University of Oregon and has been involved in coaching since 1978. He has been researching plyometric training since 1980, completing a master's thesis on jump training. In addition to authoring two books and a training video on the subject, he has written numerous articles for the National Strength and Conditioning Association and *Training & Conditioning* magazine, as well as for football, basketball, and volleyball coaching journals. He has presented the topic of explosive power training at dozens of major conferences all over the country since 1982. Radcliffe lives in Eugene, Oregon.

Bob Farentinos is the president of Farentinos Sports Enterprises Corporation in Portland, Oregon. He is a life-long competitive athlete in several sports and a seven-time national champion in cross-country skiing, specializing in 50K marathons. With a master's degree and PhD in biology, he has written extensively not only for scientific journals but for popular magazines and newspapers as well. He was a trainer for the U.S. National Ski Team and has worked with professional and Olympic cyclists, in addition to runners, rock climbers, mountaineers, ultramarathoners, and weightlifters. Farentinos lives in Portland, Oregon.

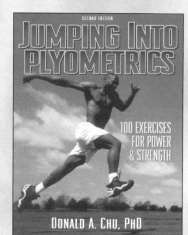

Never has there been a book like this! *Power Eating* makes it easy for athletes to add mass, cut fat, and increase strength safely, healthily, and legally. This book is loaded with the latest findings in the field—including new data on supplements and ergogenic aids. You'll find credible, research-based information such as scientific answers to common sports nutrition questions; advice on eating to increase muscle strength and power; and a complete breakdown of carbohydrate, protein, fat, and total calories for recommended foods. Also included are comprehensive sample meal plans to make it easy to map out a personal diet for maintenance, building, tapering, or cutting.

1998 • Paperback • 240 pp • Item PKLE0702
ISBN 0-88011-702-8 • $15.95 ($23.95 Canadian)

Boost your athletes' performances through explosive power training! Host Renaldo Nehemiah—former world record holder in the 110-meter high hurdles and player for the 1984 Super Bowl Champion San Francisco 49ers—presents a power-training program that will help you develop, enhance, and harness the power your athletes need to excel. In *Coaching Power*, you will learn how to develop explosive power using 24 plyometric exercises, utilize resistance training exercises to build strength, and improve speed through sprint training. Methods of combining exercises to build athlete- and sport-specific programs are included.

1999 • Item MHKV0147 • ISBN 0-7360-0147-6 • $24.95 ($37.50 Canadian)

This new edition of *Sport Stretch* is a complete guide to flexibility for both weekend warriors and elite competitors. The centerpieces of this comprehensive book are its illustrations and step-by-step guidelines for 311 different stretches. The stretches can be used individually or grouped with other stretches to form a personalized flexibility program.

This book explains the basic principles of stretching and describes how the body responds during stretching. Readers will discover what causes muscle soreness, how increased flexibility translates directly into better performance and lessens the chances of injury, and more. *Sport Stretch* also provides a selection of "All Star" stretches. These include the single best stretches for 28 muscle groups and the 12 best stretches overall. The exercises are perfect to use for warming up and cooling down.

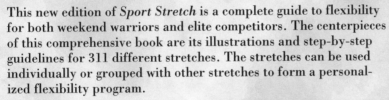

1998 • Paperback • 232 pp • Item PALT0823
ISBN 0-88011-823-7 • $15.95 ($23.95 Canadian)